INDIAN SCULPTURE AND PAINTING

INDIAN SCULPTURE
AND PAINTING

ILLUSTRATED BY TYPICAL MASTERPIECES

WITH AN EXPLANATION OF
THEIR MOTIVES AND IDEALS

BY E. B. HAVELL

AUTHOR OF "INDIAN ARCHITECTURE," "A HANDBOOK OF INDIAN ART," "A SHORT HISTORY OF INDIA," ETC.

SECOND EDITION, WITH NUMEROUS ILLUSTRATIONS

LONDON
JOHN MURRAY, ALBEMARLE STREET, W.

First Edition . . . November 1908
Second Edition 1928

PREFACE TO SECOND EDITION

THE circumstances under which this book was
written twenty years ago have, in some respects,
undergone a complete change. There has been
a remarkable growth of interest in Indian art,
both in Europe and in India, and appreciation
has grown with better knowledge. Many writers
besides myself have explored further the wonderful field of artistic research which India offers and
have added greatly to its literature. Public and
private collections of Indian sculpture and painting have been enriched, so that the material
available for study in Europe is very much larger,
and in India works of art which were commonly
regarded as worthless are now valued as they
should be. The new school of painting led by
Dr. Abanindra Nath Tagore, C.I.E., has developed
its influence vastly and helped to form a new
school of criticism with the aim of representing
the Indian point of view in the theory and practice
of the fine arts.

These changes have necessitated a thorough
revision of this pioneer work, both in the illustrations and the text. The latter has been to a

great extent rewritten, and the wealth of new
material provided by the Archæological Survey of
India, the Archæological Survey of Hyderabad,
the Victoria and Albert Museum, the British
Museum, and by private enterprise, generously
placed at my disposal, has enabled me to improve
very much the quality of many of the illustrations.

On the vital question of the preservation and
regeneration of Indian art the situation has
changed very little. Indians who have thrown
themselves with the enthusiasm of converts into
the study of their own art have shown great
ability in academic criticism and historical investi-
gation, but, following too closely the lead of
the European connoisseur, they have done very
little constructive work to prevent the extinction
of the living traditional art of India. From this
point of view the building of New Delhi, the
greatest opportunity of a century, has been a
complete fiasco, and things remain as they were
when this book was first written. On this subject,
therefore, the views formerly expressed have
required very little expansion or amendment.

I must acknowledge very warmly the kind help
I have received in providing illustrations from
Dr. F. D. K. Bosch, Director of the Archæological
Survey of Netherlands India ; Sir John Marshall,
Director-General of the Archæological Survey of
India ; Mr. G. Yazdani, Director of the Archæo-

logical Survey of Hyderabad; the Director and Secretary, Victoria and Albert Museum and Mr. C. Stanley Clarke, Curator of the Indian Section; Mr. Laurence Binyon; Mr. O. C. Gangoly, Editor of " Rupam "; Mr. Asit Kumar Haldar, Principal, Government School of Arts and Crafts, Lucknow; Mr. C. C. Holme, Editor of " The Studio "; Lady M. D. Scott-Moncrieff; and Dr. Abanindra Nath Tagore. I am under a special obligation to Mr. S. V. Ramasami Mdr. of Madras for the trouble he has taken in getting photographs of the important frescoes of Sittannavāsal.

E. B. H.

OXFORD, *October* 1927.

PREFACE TO FIRST EDITION

THE purpose of this book is artistic, not archæological ; but I have ventured to differ entirely from archæological ideas of Indian fine art, which seem to me to give a completely distorted view of the intentions of Indian artists. It is not extraordinary that these archæological conclusions have hitherto been tacitly accepted by the few European experts who have worked for art in India ; for those who are preoccupied with their own work and own ideas of art, and prejudiced by their education in Western academies, are naturally inclined to regard with complacency the influence and affluence which the present popular opinion of Indian fine art brings to them.

I do not anticipate that all my fellow-artists in Europe will at once accept the views which have forced themselves upon me gradually, and after long years of study. Having entered upon my study of Indian art with a full equipment of European academic prejudices, I know that they are not easily shaken off. No European can appreciate Indian art who does not divest himself of his Western prepossessions, endeavour to understand Indian thought, and place himself at the

Indian point of view. I am convinced that those who do so will find my artistic conclusions inevitable ; but there will always be many who believe it more interesting to use the wrong end of the telescope.

For historical and archæological facts I have consulted the best authorities, and endeavoured to avail myself of the latest researches. I have not attempted anything like a history, in the ordinary sense of the word, but an explanation. In the first attempt to deal with a subject covering so wide a field, and artistically almost unexplored, there are many difficulties. I have been obliged to leave untouched much that is necessary for a full treatment of it, but I hope I have succeeded in showing that the Indian ideal is not, as archæologists call it, a decadent and degenerate copy of a Græco-Roman prototype ; that Indian fine art is not, as an Anglo-Indian critic puts it, a form of artistic cretinism, but an opening into a new world of æsthetic thought, full of the deepest interest, and worthy of the study of all Western artists.

I hope, also, that this book may save from oblivion and from the tender mercies of the ignorant Philistine the unique collection of the Calcutta Art Gallery. I still look forward to the time when our whole administrative policy in India will be guided by intelligent and consistent views of art ; though, as the principal artistic errors in it were pointed out by Fergusson more than fifty years ago, the hope may seem to be a vain one. The ruthless vandalism which prevailed in his time has been checked. We no longer desecrate and destroy the masterpieces of the Moguls and the great monuments of ancient India : we patch them up and try to admire them. But there is still that insidious form of vandalism in our departmental system—much more cruel and deadly than active iconoclasm, because it acts through mind instead of matter—which continues blindly to crush out the means by which India might yet surpass the greatness of her ancient art.

When Great Britain's responsibility in this matter is recognised, the grievous wrong we unthinkingly do to Indian art and craft will command the attention it deserves. But my main object is to help educated Indians to a better understanding of their own national art, and to give them that faith and pride in it without which the wisest measures that any Government could devise will always be thrown away. After all, the future of Indian art is in their keeping, and they have dealt with it more cruelly than any Europeans have ever done.

Even if, for Europeans who think like Macaulay, all Indian art should be worthless, it will always remain a priceless boon for Indians, offering them something which the best European art can never give them. Let Indians of the present generation, who through Macaulay's narrow and short-sighted policy have never enjoyed this precious heritage, see that their children are put in possession of it.

I am deeply indebted to His Honour Sir Andrew Fraser, Lieutenant-Governor of Bengal, and to Mr. A. Earle, I.C.S., Director of Public Instruction, Bengal, for their sympathy and support in the publication of this book. My friend and colleague, Mr. Abanindra Nath Tagore, whose artistic work is reviewed in the last chapter, has given me valuable help by his knowledge of Sanskrit literature. I owe also acknowledgments for courteous assistance to Dr. J. D. E. Schmeltz, Director of the Ethnographic Museum, Leyden ; Mr. G. P. Rouffaer, of The Hague ; Mr. E. A. Von Saher, Director of the Colonial Museum, Haarlem ; Dr. A. K. Coomaraswamy ; Mr. Stanley Clarke, Director of the Indian Section, Victoria and Albert Museum, South Kensington ; Dr. Müller and Dr. A. von Lecoq, of the Royal Ethnographic Museum, Berlin ; Mr. F. W. Thomas, Librarian, and Mr. T. W. Arnold, Assistant Librarian, India Office ; and to Mr. E. Thurston, Superintendent, Central Museum, Madras. I must also thank Mr. W. Griggs, who has spared no efforts in the extremely difficult task of reproducing in colours the minute and delicate work of the Mogul miniature painters, and Mr. Imre G. Schwaiger, of Delhi and Simla, to whose exertions the Calcutta Art Gallery owes some of its choicest treasures.

January 1908.

CONTENTS

PART I

SCULPTURE

CHAPTER I

INTRODUCTORY

The change of attitude towards Indian art in Europe and in India—The ideals and characteristics of Indian art—Yoga and the Divine Ideal—The Himalayas in Indian art—The Indian Order of Architecture . . . . . pp. 3–15

CHAPTER II

THE EVOLUTION OF THE DIVINE IDEAL

The mystery of the Divine Form—Yantras, or geometric symbols—Early Buddhism and Yoga—Kailāsa, the nave of the universal wheel—Mahāyāna Buddhism and image-worship—The great epoch of Indian sculpture and painting—The Images of the Divine Thinker—Mathematics and æsthetics—A symbol of the Creator's Mind—Indian and Chinese images—Indian artistic anatomy—The place of the Gandhāran school in Indian art . . . . . pp. 16–28

CHAPTER III

THE EVOLUTION OF THE DIVINE IDEAL (*continued*)

The symbolism of the triangle—The Image of the Divine Mother—
Yantra and Mantra—A Sanskrit treatise on æsthetics—
Images of Tārā, the Saviouress—The Divine Power as god and
goddess—The androgynous image—The Divine Embrace—
The conflict between good and evil—Shākta philosophy and
art—Kāli . . . . pp. 29–38

CHAPTER IV

MYTHOLOGY AND METAPHYSICS

Sukrachārya on image-making—The keynote of Indian art—
Anthropomorphism in images—The Divine Form in the
Bhagavad Gītā—Multiple arms and heads—Images of Dharma-
pāla, Manjusri, and the Buddhist Trimūrti—Durgā slaying
Mahisha—Sculpture at Elephanta and Ellora—Art in India a
living force . . . . pp. 39–56

CHAPTER V

THE DANCE OF SIVA

The symbolism of the Dance—Ganesha . . . pp. 57–67

CHAPTER VI

SCHOOLS OF SCULPTURE AND PAINTING

Brahmanical influence on Buddhist art—India's unbroken tradition
—The Chola School of sculpture surviving in the present day—
The renaissance of art in India—The modern Orissa School—
A survey of Indian art and craft—A Tibetan writer on the
Indian schools of sculpture and painting . . pp. 68–79

CONTENTS

CHAPTER VII

THE HUMAN IDEAL AND THE SCULPTURES OF BHĀRHUT, SĀNCHĪ, AND AMARĀVATĪ

Indian idealism in relation to the art of everyday life—Art and education in ancient India—Art and Nature—The inspiration of Indian art—The technical characteristics of the sculptures of Bhārhut, Sānchī, and Amarāvatī—Their place in the evolution of the Indian ideal—The Amarāvatī sculptures and the influence of Gandhāran art—The ancient Indian universities the art centres of Asia . . . . . pp. 80–108

CHAPTER VIII

BOROBUDUR—THE KAILĀSA OF JAVA

The old chronicles of Java and modern archæological research—The design of Borobudur derived from the Indian stūpa—The symbolism of the stūpa—The builders' reminiscences of the pilgrimage to Kailāsa—Borobudur as the cosmic Yantra—The Dhyāni-Buddhas—The skyline of Borobudur—The sculptures of the procession path, eleven panels described and illustrated—The ethical value of Indian art . pp. 109–132

CHAPTER IX

HINDU ART IN JAVA AND CAMBODIA—PORTRAITURE

The sculptures of Prambānam—Nakhon Vat—Portraiture in Indian sculpture—Ethnical types in uncanonical religious art—Two heads of Bhima—A head of the Buddha—A horse and charioteer from Kanārak in Orissa—Image of Kuvera—A Tibetan nun—National tradition and individualism in art . . . . pp. 133–151

CONTENTS

PART II

PAINTING

CHAPTER I

INDIAN MURAL PAINTING

The great schools of mural painting—The *chitra-sālas*—Indian fresco—References to picture painting in Sanskrit literature—The Ajantā paintings, not merely an art of line—The great painting in Cave XVII—Head of Bodhisattva—The technical process of the Ajantā paintings—Modern Indian *fresco-buono*—The Sittannavāsal paintings—The Sigiri paintings—The Bagh paintings—The Ajantā tradition in modern times—Vaishnava icons—The Tibetan school — Colour symbolism—Popular pictorial art in the present day . . . pp. 155–182

CHAPTER II

PAINTING IN MOGUL TIMES

The Mongolian invasion and its effect on art—Oriental craftsmen as missionaries of civilisation—Their influence in Byzantine and Gothic art—Indian artist-missionaries in China—The rise of the Mogul school of painting—A picture by Shapur of Khurasan—Indian miniature painting in the reigns of Akbar and Jahāngīr—Rembrandt's use of Indian drawings—Shah Jahān and Aurangzīb . . . . . pp. 183–210

CHAPTER III

TYPICAL INDIAN MINIATURE PAINTINGS

Calligraphy and brush-drawing—Two brush-line drawings of Shah Jahān's school—A drawing by Ghulām—Portrait of Shah Jahān's Poet Laureate, by Bichitr—Portrait of Sultan Muhammad Kutb Shah of Golconda, by Mir Hashim—Portrait of

CONTENTS

Dara Shikoh—Ustād Mansūr and his work—Manohar—Genre
painting by Bichitr—The Hindu schools of painting—Landscape—Indian impressionism—Night and effects of artificial
light—The eighteenth century and after—Portraits of Europeans by an Indian artist—The modern tradition   pp. 211–239

CHAPTER IV

THE FUTURE OF INDIAN ART

Summary of historical development—Indian art in the nineteenth
century—Art and the universities—The Victoria Memorial
and New Delhi—The social position of Indian artists, past
and present—Art administration and its effect—Public opinion
and modern artistic taste—A renaissance of Indian painting—
The Bombay and the New Calcutta Schools—The significance
of the revival   .   .   .   .   .   .   pp. 240–277

APPENDIX

THE INDIAN PROCESS OF FRESCO BUONO   .   .   .   pp. 278–286

INDEX   .   .   .   .   pp. 287–288

2

ILLUSTRATIONS

PORTRAIT OF SULTAN MUHAMMAD KUTB SHAH OF
GOLCONDA, BY MIR HASHIM (in colours)   *Frontispiece*
From the original in the Victoria and Albert Museum.

PART I

SCULPTURE

PLATE   FACING PAGE

I. IMAGE OF THE DHYĀNI-BUDDHA, AMOGHA SIDDHA,
FROM THE NORTH SIDE OF BOROBUDUR   .   10

II. COLOSSAL IMAGE OF GAUTAMA BUDDHA, FROM ANU-
RADHAPURA, CEYLON   12

III. ALTO-RILIEVO OF THE BUDDHA PREACHING, FROM
SARNĀTH   14

IV. COPPER-GILT IMAGE OF THE BODHISATTVA PADMAPĀNI,
OR AVALOKITESHVARA (OLD NEPALESE)   .   .   16
Calcutta Art Gallery. Height 22½ in.

V. COPPER-GILT IMAGE OF VAJRAPĀNI, OR DORJE CHANG
(OLD NEPALESE)   18
Calcutta Art Gallery. Height 19 in.

VI. COPPER-GILT IMAGE OF A BODHISATTVA (MODERN
NEPALESE)   20
Calcutta Art Gallery.

VII. THE SUDARSANA-CHAKRA, OR SYMBOL OF THE CREATOR'S
MIND   20
From a photograph by the Archæological Survey of India.

VIII. BUDDHA PREACHING AT BENARES : A RELIEF FROM
LORIYĀN TANGAI (GANDHĀRAN SCHOOL)   .   .   24
From a photograph in the India Office Library.

xix

PLATE   FACING PAGE

IX. STONE IMAGE OF A BODHISATTVA FROM SARNĀTH
(EIGHTH TO NINTH CENTURY) 26
From a photograph by the Archæological Survey of India.

X. IMAGE IN COPPER (CAST) OF AVALOKITESHVARA . 26
Boston Museum of Fine Arts. Photograph by Dr. A. K. Coomaraswamy.

XI. STONE IMAGE OF AVALOKITESHVARA . . . 28
Indian Museum, Calcutta. From a photograph by the Archæological Survey of India.

XII. STONE IMAGE OF SIVA AS DAKSHINAMURTI (SOUTHERN
INDIA) 30
From a photograph by the Archæological Survey of India.

XIII. STONE IMAGE OF TĀRĀ (MEDIEVAL) . . . 32
Indian Museum, Calcutta. From a photograph by the Archæological Survey of India.

XIV. STONE IMAGE OF PRAJÑĀPĀRAMITĀ, FROM SINGHA-
SĀRI, JAVA 34
Ethnographic Museum, Leyden.

XV. HAMMERED COPPER IMAGE OF TĀRĀ (TIBET OR
NEPAL) 34
Calcutta Art Gallery. Height 15½ in.

XVI. A NĀGA AND NĀGINI 36
Indian Museum, Calcutta. From a photograph by the Archæological Survey of India.

XVII. BRONZE IMAGE OF DHARMAPĀLA 38
Batavian Museum, Java.

XVIII. HAMMERED COPPER IMAGE OF MANJUSRI . . 38
Calcutta Art Gallery. Height 11¼ in.

XIX. CAST COPPER IMAGE OF THE BUDDHIST TRIMŪRTI . 42
Calcutta Art Gallery. Height 8½ in.

XX. ALTO-RILIEVO OF DURGĀ SLAYING MAHISHA . . 44
Ethnographic Museum, Leyden.

XXI. SIVA AS BHAIRAVA : FRAGMENT FROM THE GREAT
TEMPLE, ELEPHANTA 46
From a photograph in the India Office Library.

XXII. RĀVANA UNDER KAILĀSA, FROM THE KAILĀSA
TEMPLE, ELLORA 48
From a photograph in the India Office Library.

XXIII. NARASINGHA AND HIRANYA-KĀÇIPU : A FRAGMENT
FROM THE DAS AVATĀRA CAVE AT ELLORA . 52

XXIV. SIVA AS NATĀRĀJA 58
Madras Central Museum.

PLATE   FACING PAGE

XXV. GANESHA DANCING 64
  Indian Museum, Calcutta. From a photograph by the Archæological Survey of India.

XXVI. IMAGE OF GANESHA, JAVA 66
  Ethnographic Museum, Leyden.

XXVII. THE GARDENER'S DAUGHTER, BY SHIDHARTHA MAHĀPATRA (MODERN ORISSA SCHOOL) . . 72
  From photograph supplied by Dr. Abanindra Nath Tagore, C.I.E.

XXVIII. RELIEF FROM BHĀRHUT: THE SUDARSANĀ-YAKSHINI 94
  From a photograph in the India Office Library.

XXIX. THE EASTERN GATEWAY OF THE SĀNCHĪ STŪPA (INSIDE VIEW) 96

XXX. A DRYAD FROM THE EASTERN GATEWAY, SĀNCHĪ STŪPA 96
  From a cast in the Victoria and Albert Museum.

XXXI. SCULPTURED SLAB FROM THE BASE OF THE GREAT STŪPA, AMARĀVATĪ 100
  From a photograph in the India Office Library.

XXXII. SCULPTURED SLAB FROM AMARĀVATĪ . . 102
  From the original in the British Museum.

XXXIII. RELIEF FROM THE PROCESSION PATH, BOROBUDUR, JAVA 120
  From a photograph by Mr. Van Kinsbergen.

XXXIV. RELIEF FROM THE PROCESSION PATH, BOROBUDUR, JAVA 122
  From a photograph by Mr. Van Kinsbergen.

XXXV. RELIEF FROM THE PROCESSION PATH, BOROBUDUR, JAVA 124
  From a photograph by Mr. Van Kinsbergen.

XXXVI. RELIEF FROM THE PROCESSION PATH, BOROBUDUR, JAVA 126
  From a photograph by Mr. Van Kinsbergen.

XXXVII. RELIEF FROM THE PROCESSION PATH, BOROBUDUR, JAVA 128
  From a photograph by Mr. Van Kinsbergen.

XXXVIII. RELIEF FROM THE PROCESSION PATH, BOROBUDUR, JAVA 128
  From a photograph by Mr. Van Kinsbergen.

XXXIX. RĀMĀYANA RELIEF, PRAMBĀNAM, JAVA . . 134
  From a photograph by the Archæological Survey of Netherlands India.

PLATE   FACING PAGE

XL. RĀMĀYANA RELIEF, PRAMBĀNAM, JAVA . . 136
   From a photograph by the Archæological Survey of Netherlands India.

XLI. TWO HEADS FROM THE BHIMA TEMPLE, ON THE
   DIENG PLATEAU, JAVA 142

XLII. HEAD OF THE BUDDHA 144
   From the original in the Ethnographic Museum, Java.

XLIII. HORSE AND CHARIOTEER, KANĀRAK, ORISSA . 146
   From a photograph in the India Office Library.

XLIV. GILT-COPPER IMAGE OF KUVERA . . . 148
   From the original in the Calcutta Art Gallery.

XLV. GILT-COPPER STATUETTE OF A TIBETAN NUN . 150
   From the original in the Calcutta Art Gallery. Height 10 in.

PART II
PAINTING

XLVI. THE BUDDHA'S RETURN TO HIS HOME: PAINTING
   IN ANTECHAMBER, CAVE XVII, AJANTĀ . 166
   From a photograph by the Archæological Department, Hyderabad

XLVIA. SKETCH SHOWING THE FULL DESIGN AND PRO-
   PORTIONS OF THE PAINTING 166

XLVII. YASODHARĀ AND RĀHULA: DETAIL FROM THE
   PAINTING OF THE BUDDHA'S RETURN . . 168
   From a photograph by the Archæological Department, Hyderabad.

XLVIII. HEAD OF BODHISATTVA, FROM THE PAINTING IN
   CAVE I, AJANTĀ 170
   From a photograph taken for M. Victor Goloubeff.

XLIX. MODERN MURAL DECORATION IN INDIAN *fresco
   buono* 172
   Entrance hall of the Calcutta School of Art.

L. PAINTING AT SITTANNAVĀSAL 174
   From a photograph by Mr. S. Raja.

LI. TWO PAINTINGS FROM SIGIRI, CEYLON (FIFTH
   CENTURY) 176
   From photographs by the Archæological Survey of Ceylon.

LII. A GROUP FROM THE GREAT FRESCO OF THE RANG
   MAHALL, BAGH 176
   From a copy by Mr. Asit Kumar Haldar.

PLATE   FACING PAGE

LIII. THE BIRTH CEREMONY OF THE INFANT KRISHNA 178
Kangra School brush drawing, eighteenth [or nineteenth century, Author's Collection.

LIV. THE CORONATION OF RĀMA AND SĪTĀ . . 180
From a painting in the Calcutta Art Gallery.

LV. A NAUTCH PARTY AT THE COURT OF MUHAMMAD TUGLAK, BY SHAPUR OF KHURASAN . . 194
From a painting in the Calcutta Art Gallery.

LVI. TWO BRUSH-LINE PORTRAITS, SCHOOL OF SHAH JAHĀN 208
Lady M. D. Scott-Moncrieff's Collection.

LVII. PRINCE MUHAMMAD MURAD ON THE ELEPHANT IQBAL, DRAWN BY GHULĀM, A.D. 1610 . 214
From a shaded brush drawing in the Calcutta Art Gallery.

LVIII. MUHAMMAD JAM QUDSI, SHAH JAHĀN'S POET LAUREATE, BY BICHITR (in colours) . . 216
From a coloured brush drawing in the Calcutta Art Gallery.

LIX. PRINCE DĀRĀ SHIKOH 218
From the original in the Victoria Memorial Collection, Calcutta.

LX. A TURKEY-COCK, BY USTĀD MANSŪR . . 220
From the original in the Calcutta Art Gallery.

LXI. TWO SĀRAS, BY USTĀD MANSŪR . . . 222
From the original in the Victoria and Albert Museum.

LXII. A BLACK BUCK, BY MANOHAR . . . 224
From the original in the British Museum.

LXIII. THE TAMBURA PLAYER, BY BICHITR (in colours) 226
From the original in the Victoria and Albert Museum.

LXIV. BĀZ BAHĀDUR AND RŪP MATI . . . 228
From the original in the Calcutta Art Gallery.

LXV. DEER-HUNTING BY NIGHT . . . 230
From the original in the Calcutta Art Gallery.

LXVI. TRAVELLERS ROUND A CAMP-FIRE . . 232
From the original in the Calcutta Art Gallery.

LXVII. IN A ZANANA GARDEN (in colours) . . 234
From an unfinished painting in the Author's Collection.

LXVIII. A MUSIC PARTY (in colours) . . . 236
From a modern painting in the Author's Collection.

PLATE   FACING PAGE

LXIX. PORTRAIT OF AN ANGLO-INDIAN OF THE GEORGIAN
      PERIOD 238
      From a brush drawing in the Calcutta Art Gallery.

LXX. PORTRAITS OF ANGLO-INDIANS OF THE GEORGIAN
     PERIOD 238
     From brush drawings in the Calcutta Art Gallery.

LXXI. KĀCHA AND DEVĀJĀNI, A FRESCO PAINTING BY
      ABANINDRA NATH TAGORE 244
      From the original in the Calcutta Art Gallery.

LXXII. ILLUSTRATION TO THE RUBÁIYÁT OF OMAR
       KHAYYÁM, BY ABANINDRA NATH TAGORE (in
       colours) 248
       *From the original in the Author's Collection, by permission of the Pro-
       prietors of the Studio, owners of the copyright.*

LXXIII. THE END OF THE JOURNEY, PAINTED BY ABAN-
        INDRA NATH TAGORE 254

LXXIV. SIVA-SĪMANTINĪ, PAINTED BY ABANINDRA NATH
       TAGORE 260

LXXV. THE TRIAL OF THE PRINCES, PAINTED BY NANDA
      LAL BOSE 266

LXXVI. SATI, PAINTED BY NANDA LAL BOSE . . 270

LXXVII. RĀSA LĪLĀ, PAINTED BY ASIT KUMAR HALDAR 274

LXXVIII. THE FLIGHT OF LAKSHMAN SEN, PAINTED BY
         SURENDRA NATH GANGULY 276

INSETS

FIG.   PAGE

1. HOLLOW YANTRA FROM BOROBUDUR, CONTAINING AN
   IMAGE OF A DHYĀNI-BUDDHA 23

2. A YANTRA IN TWO DIMENSIONS (*Śrīchakra*) . . 23

3. A YANTRA IN THREE DIMENSIONS, CUT IN CRYSTAL . 23

4. SKYLINE OF BOROBUDUR 114

PART I

SCULPTURE

CHAPTER I

INTRODUCTORY

" Quand on veut comprendre un art, il faut regarder l'âme du public auquel il s'adressait."—H. TAINE, " Voyage en Italie."

IT is *prima facie* incredible that a highly developed civilisation, spreading over thousands of years and over a vast area like India, which has produced a splendid literature and expressed lofty ideals in building materials, should have lacked the capacity, or found no occasion, for giving them expression in sculpture and painting. Nevertheless, when this book was first published, twenty years ago, such was the general opinion of European savants and art critics. It was an hypothesis which had governed our whole educational policy in India since universities, museums, art galleries, and schools of art were established under British rule.

Quotations from many eminent European writers illustrating this point of view were given in the first edition of this book, but it is unnecessary to reprint them now or to recall the contemptuous phrases with which an ardent

3

admirer of Indian craftsmanship, Sir George Birdwood, author of the official handbook to the Indian section of the Victoria and Albert Museum, ridiculed the Indian artist's divine ideal. He, like Ruskin and other Victorian critics, held that " the unfettered and impassioned realisation of the ideals kindled within us by the things without us " was beyond the capacity of the Indian craftsman. Indian art to him meant no more than a pretty chintz, a rich brocade, or gorgeous carpet, fantastic carving, or curious inlay ; and an ancient architecture fascinating to the archæologist and tourist with its reminiscences of bygone pomp and splendour, but an extinct art useless for the needs and ideals of our prosaic and practical times.

The years which have passed since this controversy began have seen a remarkable change in the attitude of European critics towards Indian art generally, though to India's grievous injury her mistress art still remains under the blighting influence of Victorian prejudice. The capacity of Indian builders for creative work is still belittled and derided, but it is no longer necessary to urge the claims of Indian sculptors and painters of bygone days to be regarded as artists rather than as purveyors of ethnological curiosities. Judging by commercial values Indian sculpture and painting appear to have an insignificant importance compared with the works of European masters, but it is a healthy sign that a new school of artistic criticism has arisen in India which seeks to appraise Indian art by its own standards rather than by the opinions of the market-place or by the verdict of European assessors, not often entirely disinterested.

Yet it must be borne in mind that the careful classification of Indian art into schools and ritualistic categories, a work which is now pursued with so much interest by Indian and European scholars, is likely to lead no further than the former attitude of indifference or contempt, unless it is realised that Indian art is the true expression of Indian life and of religion as the interpretation of life, not merely an æsthetic formula which the student can learn by heart. To connect it with its own natural environment, to follow its actual practice in the present day, will bring us nearer to its inspirational sources than the study of its ritualistic canons, or the search for its æsthetic prescriptions in Sanskrit texts.

For, as Mr. Laurence Binyon has well said, the supreme æsthetic quality of the great religious art of India lies in the fact that it is not self-conscious. " Design, colour composition, all the purely artistic elements of their work, were left to the more intuitive activities of the mind . . . it solves difficult problems not by scientifically working out a theory but simply—*ambulando.*

Our most modern art tortures itself in its austere quest of a purely æsthetic aim. But it is a perplexing paradox of human nature that to choose a certain aim and to consciously pursue it rarely ends in perfect accomplishment of that aim : if the aim is reached it is at the cost of impoverishment."

Until the nineteenth century India has solved all her artistic problems in her own simple way— *ambulando*. Her ancient Aryan culture, a great philosophic synthesis covering the whole field of human endeavour, went on century after century enriching itself and all the races entering the Aryan pale with new experiences of life. The fury of iconoclasts who sought to destroy it by violence only gave new impulses to artistic creation, so that at the beginning of the nineteenth century Indian art was more varied in its local developments than the whole art of Europe, though in all this variety of formal expression it preserved its essential spiritual unity, the religious instinct which is ever its vital force.

It is true, as Mr. Binyon has said, that in the great art of India the religious import was everything to the artists ; they generally consecrated their lives to religion as many great European artists have done. But this does not imply that they turned away their eyes from the facts and phenomena of nature and made themselves incapable of rendering them truthfully, as Ruskin and many lesser critics have asserted. Indian artists were not ascetics who shut themselves out of the world, but mystics who communed with Nature to find the secret of the universal life.

The common philosophic basis of art in all countries assumes that art is not merely an imitation or record of facts and phenomena in Nature, but an interpretation—the effort of the human mind to grasp the inner beauty and meaning of the external facts of Nature. To the European Nature is always an obvious reality which must be studied, exploited, and analysed, so that the exact composition of every organic and inorganic element in it may be ascertained and explained.

" The modern citizen," as Taine says, " is constrained to confine himself to the little province of a specialist. One development excludes the others : he must be a professional man, politician, or savant, a man of business or a family man—he must shut himself up in one occupation and cut himself off from the others : he would be insufficient if he were not mutilated. For this reason he has lost his tranquillity, and art is deprived of its harmony. Moreover, the sculptor speaks no more to a religious city, but to a crowd of inquisitive individuals ; he ceases to be, for his part, citizen and priest—he is only a man and artist. He insists upon the anatomical detail which will attract the connoisseur and on the striking expression which will be understood by the ignorant. He is a superior kind of shop-keeper, who wishes to compel public attention and to keep it. He makes a simple work of art, and not a work of national art. The spectator pays him in praise and he pays the spectator in pleasure." [1]

Viewed from this secularist and pseudo-scientific angle, Indian art will always be unattractive and incomprehensible. But the Indian artist is not really blind to the beauties of Nature. He can be realistic in the European sense, though realism for him has a different meaning to that which we attach to it, for the philosophy which inspires him regards all that we see in nature as transitory, illusive phenomena, and declares that the only Reality is the Divine Essence or Spirit. Thus while modern European art hardly concerns itself with the Unseen, but limits its mental range to the realm of Nature and thus retains, even in its highest flights, the sense and form of its earthly environment, Indian art (like the Egyptian, of which it is the living representative) is always striving to realise something of the universal, the eternal, and the infinite.

European art, since the so-called Renaissance, has, as it were, its wings clipped : it knows only the beauty of earthly things. Indian art, soaring into the highest empyrean, is ever trying to

[1] " Voyage en Italie," vol. ii, p. 165.

bring down to earth something of the beauty of the things above.

The Greeks and the artists of the Renaissance who followed in their footsteps attempted to arrive at a scientific standard of beauty by a selection of what appeared to them most admirable in various types of humanity and in natural forms and appearances. Physical beauty attained by martial exercises was to the Greeks a divine characteristic : the perfect human animal received divine honours both before and after death. The Indian artist had an entirely different starting-point. He considered that the perfect human animal was an inadequate symbol for the beauty of the divine nature which comprehended all human qualities and transcended them all. It was only by meditating on the Ultimate Perfection that the artist's mind could perceive some glimmer of the beauty of the Godhead.

Mere bodily strength and mundane perfections of form are never glorified in Indian art. When the Indian artist models a representation of the Deity with an attenuated waist and suppresses all the smaller anatomical details so as to obtain an extreme simplicity of contour, the European draws a mental comparison with the ideas of Phidias or Michelangelo and declares that the Indian is sadly ignorant of anatomy and incapable of imitating the higher forms of nature.

But the Indian artist in the best period of

3

Indian sculpture and painting was no more
ignorant of anatomy than Phidias or Praxiteles.
He would create a higher and more etherealised
type than a Grecian athlete or a Roman senator,
and suggest that spiritual beauty which according
to his philosophy can only be reached by the
surrender of worldly attachments and the suppression of worldly desires.

Indian art is essentially idealistic, mystic,
symbolic, and transcendental. The artist is both
priest and poet. In this respect Indian art is
closely allied to the Gothic art of Europe—
indeed, Gothic art is only the Eastern consciousness manifesting itself in a Western environment.
But while the Christian art of the Middle Ages is
always emotional, rendering literally the pain of
the mortification of the flesh, the bodily sufferings
of the Man of Sorrows, Indian art appeals more
to the imagination and strives to realise the
spirituality and abstraction of a supra-terrestrial
sphere.

Indian mysticism had its philosophic system,
the Yoga-sāstra ; Yoga was not and is not
practised merely as a spiritual exercise leading
to the beatific vision. It claims to be a psychological process of drawing into oneself the dyna-
mis or the logos which controls the universe and
to be adaptable for all kinds of mental and
physical activity. It inspired the artist, poet,
and musician as well as the mystic who sought

PLATE I

pyramid

THE DHYĀNI-BUDDHA, AMOGHA SIDDHA, BOROBUDUR

spiritual enlightenment. It gave the craftsman his creative skill and the soldier perfect control over his weapons, the statesman his far-seeing vision, the seer and inspired thinker his supernatural powers.

Indian art thus deifies the power of mind over matter in the figure of the Perfect Yogi, the Divine Thinker, one which is commonly associated with Buddhism only, but is really a concept common to all schools of Indian theism. The attempt to trace the source of its inspiration exclusively from the artistic rendering of Buddhist legends, more especially from the efforts of the Græco-Baktrian school which was more or less foreign to India, has led to hopeless confusion and misconception of the motives of Indian artists. For the indigenous art of India is a great synthesis embracing many different theological and mythological elements, but inspired by a common ideal.

The historical Buddha was an adept in Yoga and through Yoga attained enlightenment. But when he was deified in Mahāyāna Buddhism, he was transfigured in Indian eyes as the Divine Yogi of the Himalayas, who in the form of a white elephant, the genius loci of the mountains, had entered the womb of Māyā and had been born on earth as the Prince Siddhartha. At the moment when as a sannyasin practising Yoga he attained enlightenment his divine nature was manifested in an apparition shining like gold purified of its earthly dross, with limbs rounded and smooth-skinned like a woman's, but with the massive neck and shoulders and narrow waist of an Indian hero—an abstract of Universal Form and a symbol of spiritual strength transcending human thought.

This was the common ideal for all images of the Divine Thinker whatever their special sectarian connotation might be. It appears under the names of different Buddhas and Bodhisattvas, of Brahmā, Vishnu, or Siva, of Mahāvīra and other Jain Tirthankaras. The Græco-Baktrian artists of Gandhāra caught a faint glimmer of the idea, but generally represented the divine Buddha as an Indo-Grecian Apollo or as a monk practising his daily *sādhana* within the walls of a Gandhāran monastery (Plate VIII). European critics poring over museum specimens and convinced that Indian artists, as Ruskin said, wilfully sealed up for themselves the book of life, have seized upon this commonplace academic prescription as the inspiring motive of the Indian divine ideal, to worship which pilgrims of all sects still climb the long and perilous ascent to the innermost recesses of the Himalayas.

In all Indian poetry, art, and mythology, the sublime nature of the Himalayas has always been regarded as a special revelation of divine beauty and as a fitting shrine for all the gods. On Mt. Kailāsa, the temple's glorious pinnacle, sits the

PLATE II

GAUTAMA BUDDHA

(From Anuradhapura, Ceylon)

Divine Thinker in His icy cell, controlling the
Universe by the power of Yoga. Here Vyāsa,
says the Mahābhārata, taught the Vedas to his
disciples. Here is the heavenly staircase by
which the Lord Buddha and many other Avatars
descended to be born on earth, and here the
heavenly Ganges falls in seven torrents over the
mountain's crest. The sacred lake, Mānasarovara, fed by Kailāsa's snows, is the legendary
source of the four world-rivers which water the
four great continents, or the four petals of the
World Lotus, another pregnant symbol in Indian
art. The wild geese (*hamsas*) which drift thither
with the monsoon winds, are to the pious Hindu
symbols of the human soul winging its way to its
heavenly resting-place.

The lake itself, " the most excellent Lake of the
Mind," was physically the symbol of fertility,
the Creator's Well whose perennial overflow was
the world's life-stream. In Indian art, as in the
classical art of Europe, mountains, rivers, and
lakes were personified into deities, but the essential difference between the Indian and the Western
outlook is that the Indian artistic symbol is not
merely an æsthetic formula. The physical appearance, Nature herself, is always charged with
spiritual significance; the idealism of the Vedas
is the life and soul of Indian art. Thus the
Creator's Himalayan well, the natural symbol,
becomes the divine receptacle of the universal

mind-force, *manas*, the lotus-jar holding the essence of purity, the nectar of immortality, *amrita*, which Vishnu churned from the Cosmic Ocean. The four world-rivers became the four Vedas, revealed to Indian seers on that holy spot.

In the classical Western orders of architecture, which official city builders regard as the most appropriate symbols of British achievements in India, the Corinthian capital—apart from its architectonic purpose—is merely a pleasing composition of acanthus leaves and volutes; the Tuscan, Doric, and Ionic only harmonious arrangements of mouldings and ornaments. If they meant more to the Greeks and Romans we have lost their feeling. The Indian builder in creating his symbolic order struck a deeper and more spiritual note; a suggestion of the glorious Himalayan vision which was ever present in his mind. The Himalayas formed the resplendent pillar of the heavenly vault, holding aloft as its capital the precious lotus-jar of immortality guarded by the lions of the four quarters and by the Devas who won it in conflict with the powers of evil. This was the motif, drawn from India's own fount of inspiration, which the Indian craftsman with inexhaustible fantasy and power of adaptation has used for palace and mansion, temple and mosque, reception hall and council chamber from before the time of Asoka down to the present day. Whatever may be the æsthetic

PLATE III

THE BUDDHA PREACHING

(From Sarnāth)

(poor)
weak joints

value of the Western formula which modern departmentalism forces on the Indian craftsman, it can never be worth the loss to the world's art implied in the drying up of India's own inspirational sources, and the extinction of the great living tradition in which she expresses her spiritual ideals. The stagnant pool of a dead classicism from which even Christian churches in India seek to draw their æsthetic inspiration will not bring about a renaissance of art or a reawakening of India's spiritual life.

CHAPTER II

THE EVOLUTION OF THE DIVINE IDEAL

INDIAN artists for many centuries shrank from the thought of depicting for the common crowd the Yogi's vision of the Divine Form : like the secret lore of the Vedas it was a sacred mystery revealed to none but the elect. Even the Brahman versed in the philosophy of the Upanishads looked upon the Yogi's vision as an imperfect revelation of the Godhead which embraced all forms and transcended them all. The geometric forms used in Vedic ritual seemed to him more appropriate symbols of universal powers than any icons suggestive of human limitations, and to this day *yantras*, or geometric symbols, are used in higher Brahmanical ritual in preference to images of the Hindu pantheon (Figs. 2 and 3).

The primitive Buddhist Church did not hold with the practice of Yoga as a means of divine revelation. Meditation (*dhyāna*), which was the Buddhist equivalent of Yoga, was not for absorbing the nature of the Godhead but for instilling in the mind of the faithful the principles of

PLATE IV

PADMAPĀNI, OLD NEPALESE

(Calcutta Art Gallery)

the moral law which ruled the universe. The great Teacher of the Law had returned to his Himalayan abode whence he came and was now invisible. Early Buddhist artists were realists like the great Flemish masters, representing the miraculous as events of ordinary life, but following the Master's teaching they made no attempt to penetrate behind the veil. The mystical element characteristic of Indian iconography in its full artistic maturity does not on this account become prominent in the early Buddhist monuments, though the symbolical method of representing the Himalayas as the World Pillar supporting the Wheel of the Law appears as the principal motive of architectural structure. Fragmentary as the records of early Indian art are, they show that Buddhists did not cease to regard the Himalayas as the holiest of holy ground. Kapilavastu, Bodh-Gāyā, Sarnāth, and Kuçināgara were sanctified by the Master's footsteps in his final incarnation. But the end of the great northern pilgrimage was still Kailāsa, as it had been for the seers of Vedic times and for the heroes of the Mahābhārata. Kailāsa was the nave of the universal wheel, the focus of world forces, and even now the Buddhist pilgrim worships the mountain as the heavenly mansion of Buddhas and Bodhisattvas, while the Hindu sees in it the hermitage of the Divine Yogi, Siva.

When Buddhism in its Mahāyāna development

became a definite theology, image-worship was
not only tolerated but became an essential part
of its *sādhana*. At the same time the philosophy
of Buddhism adapted itself to the Brahmanical
theory of Yoga and the natural desire of the
devout Buddhist to worship the image of the
Divine Yogi without the perilous climb to the
heights of Kailāsa was gratified, for the temple
artist was assumed to be able to transport himself
by Yoga to the Tusita heavens and bring back a
faithful portrait of the Blessed One.

Thus India's dream of the Universal Form
which she had so long kept secret gradually
materialised as the great epoch of Indian sculpture
and painting began to dawn. At the beginning
of the Christian Era and for some centuries
previously, when the classic art of Europe had
already passed its zenith, India was drawing in
towards herself a great flood of artistic culture
from Western Asia, derived originally from the
far-distant sources of Babylonia and Assyria, but
strongly tinged with the subsidiary stream which
was then flowing into it from Greece and Rome.
Out of these eclectic influences, joined with the
old indigenous traditions, Indian religious thought
quickly formulated a new synthesis of art, which
in its turn became the source from which other
currents flowed north, south, east, and west.

In the early centuries of the Christian era and
from this Indian source came the inspiration of

PLATE V

VAJRAPĀNI, OR DORJE CHANG, OLD NEPALESE

(Calcutta Art Gallery)

the great schools of Chinese painting which from the seventh to the thirteenth centuries stood first in the whole world. Successive hordes of Asiatic invaders, beginning with those which flocked like vultures to gather the spoil of the decaying Roman empire, kept open the highways between East and West and brought a reflex of the same traditions into Europe.

From the seaports of her eastern and western coasts streams of Indian colonists, missionaries, and craftsmen poured all over Southern Asia, Ceylon, Burma, Siam, Sumatra, Java, and far-distant Cambodia. Through China and Korea, Indian art entered Japan about the middle of the sixth century.

The Indian ideal came to fruition in the great religious sagas, the Mahābhārata and Rāmāyana, in Sakuntala and other masterpieces of the Sanskrit drama, in colossal schemes of temple sculpture, inspired by the work of the divine craftsman, Vishvakarma, who built the heavenly temple of the snows, and in many a frescoed court and hall the splendour of which can only be dimly realised in the fragments of Ajantā, Bagh, and Sigiri. And just as the many vernacular versions of the Sanskrit epics made the story of the Pāndava heroes and Rāma's romance as familiar to the common folk in India's eastern colonies as they were to the court bards of Indraprashta and Ayodhyā, so the image of the Divine Thinker

of Kailāsa took a local shape and significance
nearer to or farther from the original Himalayan
concept, according to the cult which used it
and its particular environment. The Buddhist
sculptors of Gandhāra Hellenised it for their
royal Kushān patrons, just as Christian artists
gave Biblical scenes a local colour. China, Japan,
Siam, Java, and Cambodia made it their own.
Yet in each local re-shaping of the image some
memory, faint or vivid, of the Indian ideal arche-
type lingers. Gandhāra knew the Divine
Buddha's Himalayan shrine, for the famous relic
casket of Kanishka's great stūpa at Peshawar
shows the Buddha enthroned on the " seed-vessel
of the World-Lotus " and the sacred geese flying
round it. Java gave her mountains Himalayan
names, and her greatest monument, Borobudur,
is her Kailāsa.

Though the concept of the Divine Thinker
must be said to be Indian, or Hindu, rather than
Buddhist, by far the greatest number of classical
examples of the image belong to Buddhism. The
illustrations, Plates I to VI, show fine Buddhist
examples dating from about the fourth century
A.D., when the image assumed its most perfect
Indian form, down to modern times. To find its
proper place in Indian artistic thought one must
look beyond its incidental legendary, mythological, or ritualistic associations and connect it
with the primeval Indian ideal, the gigantic figure

PLATE VI

A BODHISATTVA, MODERN NEPALESE

(Calcutta Art Gallery)

PLATE VII

THE SUDARSANA-CHAKRA

of the Deity enthroned on the world's highest snow-peak and revealing Himself in the glory of a Himalayan sunrise or sunset. This was the divine image which the Indian artist brought down to earth and used as a standard of physical perfection to which men as well as gods could attain by mental rather than by physical effort.

The wonderful Buddha of Anuradhapura, Plate II, is one of the few colossal images of early Gupta times which escaped the Muhammadan iconoclast. It was probably executed in the first half of the fourth century A.D., in the reign of King Meghadarma of Ceylon, by a sculptor from northern India. It represents the Buddha just emerging from the Yoga trance, the left leg being released from the " adamantine " pose of profound meditation, when both legs are firmly locked together. In modern times a false note of naturalism has been given to it by placing it under a real bodhi-tree, but originally it must have formed part of a great architectural scheme, like that of Borobudur, more in keeping with the idealism of the image. For the artist had no intention of showing the emaciated body of the Sakyan monk reduced to a living skeleton by a prolonged fast, as the Gandhāran sculptors some-times vulgarly portrayed it—but the tremendous apparition of the Divine Yogi of the Himalayas which flashed upon the world when the En-lightened One attained Nirvana.

The worshipper saw also a symbolic meaning in the design of the image, regarded as pure form. In Plate I it will be seen that the contours of the front view of the Dhyāni[1]-Buddha fit as closely as possible into a triangle ; the whole figure approximates to a pyramidal shape. In the great temple of Borobudur where this Dhyāni-Buddha was placed, the builders elaborated the geometric symbolism by enclosing the image in a hollow, bell-shaped stone cupola, or dagoba, pierced by lattice-work formed by a row of

---

[1] " The term Dhyāna (Jñāna) is a general expression for the four gradations of mystic meditation which have ethereal spaces or worlds corresponding to them, and a Dhyāni-Buddha is a Buddha who is supposed to exist as a kind of spiritual essence in those higher regions of abstract thought. That is to say, every Buddha who appears on earth in a temporal body—with the object of teaching men how to gain Nirvana—exists also in an ideal counterpart, or ethereal representation of himself in these formless worlds of meditation. These ideal Buddhas are as numerous as the human Buddhas, but as there are only five chief human Buddhas in the present age—Kraka-chandra, Kanika-muni, Kāsyapa, Gautama, and the future Buddha, Maitreya, so there are only five corresponding Dhyāni-Buddhas—Vairoćana, Akshobhya, Ratnasambhava, Amitabha, and Amogha-siddha (sometimes represented in images as possessing a third eye). But this is not all. Each of them produces, by a process of evolution, a kind of emanation from himself called a Dhyāni-Bodhisattva, to act as the practical head and guardian of the Buddhist community between the death of each human Buddha and the advent of his successor. Hence there are five Bodhisattvas—Samanta-bhadra, Vajrapāni, Ratnapāni, Pad mapāni (Avalokiteshvara), and Vīsvapāni—corresponding to the five Dhyāni-Buddhas, and to the five earthly Buddhas respectively. In Nepal five corresponding female Shaktis or Tārā-devīs are named."
—Sir M. Monier-Williams, " Buddhism," pp. 202–3.

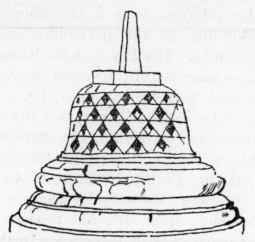

FIG. 1.—Hollow yantra at Borobudur containing
an image of a Dhyāni-Buddha.

Bindu.

FIG. 3.—A yantra in three
dimensions cut in crystal
(Bindu on the top), used
in Hindu ritual. From
the original in the collection of Sir John Wood-
roffe.

FIG. 2.—A yantra in two dimensions
used in Hindu ritual.

intersecting triangles through the interstices of which the pilgrims viewed the image of the Dhyāni-Buddha, as the personification of the cosmic pyramid. The Hindu, accustomed to the geometric symbolism of the *yantra* in his religious ritual, would perceive at once the sculptor's meaning. The dagoba (Fig. 1) was the *yantra* of three dimensions representing the universe of pure form out of which the world-lotus evolved. Within sat the Divine Inventor of the cosmic machine blessing His worshippers.

Hindu iconographic art, like modern cubism, joins mathematics with æsthetics. In the *yantra* (Figs. 2 and 3) it shows the impersonal form of the Godhead developing mathematically from a central point (Bindu). In the corresponding icon it reveals the personal aspect of the deity, or *devata*, evolving from the impersonal. Modern Hindu ritual gives an interesting analogy with the geometric symbolism of the Borobudur Dhyāni-Buddha. The principal object of worship in Vaishnava temples in Southern India is the Sudarśana Chakra, Vishnu's discus, which symbolises the Creator's mind, or the first thought of the Supreme Being when the desire of Creation moved Him to manifest Himself. It is represented as a circle of fire (Plate VII) with four projecting points of flame. On one face of the chakra sits the Lion incarnation of Vishnu in Yogi pose enclosed in an equilateral triangle. On the other

BUDDHA PREACHING AT BENARES

(Gandhāran School)

24]

face are two similar triangles, one standing on its apex and the other on its base, symbolising respectively the evolutionary and involutionary cosmic powers. This is the mystic symbol of the universe known as King Solomon's Seal. Within it stands the figure of Vishnu in his Boar incarnation—the one in which he raised the earth from the Flood. He is armed at all points with his spiritual weapons with which he destroys *avidya*, or ignorance regarded as the source of all evil.

When the figure of the Divine Yogi is thus seen with its Himalayan background and placed in its proper metaphysical or religious environment the austerity and formality of design characteristic of Indian classical types seem to be not only appropriate but inevitable, even if the suavity and charm of Chinese and Japanese images may be more attractive to the Western mind. The Buddha image came to China and Japan through Gandhāra, and in this new environment the austere Yogi of Kailāsa was transformed into the benignant guardian spirit of a delightful monastic garden. Thus the aloofness and mystery of the Indian pilgrim's ideal were generally foreign to the art of China and Japan.

Chinese and Indian influences are blended in the fine gilt copper image of the Bodhisattva Padmapāni, or Avalokiteshvara, " the Lord who looks down with pity," who is the guardian deity of Tibet (Plate IV). The image is entirely built up

4

of hammered copper ; the tiara and other ornaments are set with rubies, turquoise, lapis, and
crystal. The beautiful modelling of the hands is
especially noticeable. It is probably of Nepalese
workmanship, date uncertain. More typically
Indian is the very exquisite Nepalese image of
Dorje Chang, or the Bodhisattva Vajrapāni,
" the Wielder of the Thunderbolt," seated on his
lotus-throne. This is also of hammered copper-
gilt, perhaps seventeenth-century work. The tradition of the Divine Yogi survives in the modern
art of Nepal, of which the cast copper-gilt image
of a Bodhisattva, Plate VI, is a good example.
Though inferior in execution it has the same fine
feeling as the earlier art. It is distinguished by
the graceful conventionalisation of the bodhi-
tree, disposed as a wreath round the Bodhisattva, who holds in his hand the jar of amrita,
the nectar of immortality. At the foot of the
pedestal are the figures of the three devotees
who have dedicated the image to some Nepalese
or Tibetan shrine.

Many European critics, applying the academic
prescriptions of Europe to Indian art without
recognising its intentions and ideals, have attributed to the imagers of the divine form a deplorable lack of anatomical knowledge. They have
assumed that Indian artists, with the best opportunities in the world of studying the nude, were
too ignorant and uncultured to draw or model the

PLATE IX

A BODHISATTVA FROM SARNĀTH

PLATE X

AVALOKITESHVARA

(Boston Museum of Fine Arts)

human form as it appears to the eye, and were content to make themselves feeble copyists of the models provided for them by the Gandhāran school. The criticism is quite pointless when the finest examples of Indian sculpture and painting are considered. The best Indian sculptors and painters did not fail in technical accomplishment, even in comparison with European standards. In the idealised image of the divine form the bony structure of the body and limbs and the mechanism of the joints are perfectly understood, even though the muscular system is purposely simplified to express the artist's ideal. Neither was the Indian artist tied down to one rigid formula of the divine ideal, though the static pose of the Yogi wholly absorbed in meditation gave the keynote of his symbolism. The ritualistic poses prescribed for the Mahāyānist and Brahmanical pantheons became so numerous and varied that the temple artist would have had ample scope for his creative powers, as well as for his technical skill in rendering the form and action of the human body, even if a rich mythology had not provided him with other subjects. The two Bodhisattvas, Plates IX and XI, and the monumental image of Siva, Plate XII, in which the human side of the divine ideal is more prominent, are as perfect in the pure technique of contour and surface modelling as they are great in the rhythmic design of the figure and the balanced harmony of the decorative setting. The Dancing Siva, Plate XXIV, is a well-known example of a very difficult movement rendered with perfect anatomical accuracy. Such high technical accomplishment is by no means exceptional in Indian hieratic art, though there is sometimes a tendency to render the ideal beauty of the Perfect Yogi with poverty of plastic technique, flabbiness of surface modelling, and bad articulation of the joints. Some of this weakness is shown in the Sarnāth Buddha, Plate III, found near the spot where the Buddha preached his first sermon. It is evidently a Gupta craftsman's copy of some famous imager's masterpiece. Such copies, good, bad, and indifferent, were doubtless made in prodigious numbers, and the tendency of a copyist is always to exaggerate the defects of the master's qualities. The discriminating critic will not discern in such defects the essential characteristic of the Indian divine ideal. Nor will he fail to place the Gandhāran School in its true place as a somewhat trivial local development in Indian art, a side current originating in political rather than artistic sources which was quickly absorbed into the main stream of Indian thought proceeding from its original Vedic ideal.

PLATE XI

AVALOKITESHVARA

(Indian Museum)

CHAPTER III

THE EVOLUTION OF THE DIVINE IDEAL (*continued*)

PERFECT knowledge, or abstract thought, regarded as the male principle and imaged in Indian art in the figure of the Divine Yogi, though it contains within Itself the germ of all things, remains inert without the will and power to create, which imply a cosmic energy, or *Shakti*. An equilateral triangle is the geometric symbol of the three co-ordinated cosmic powers, Will (Ichchā), Knowledge (Jnāna), and Action (Kriya), or the Three Aspects of the One, embodied in the Divine Form. When standing on its base the triangle symbolises the male principle ; on its apex the female principle.[1] The two triangles intersecting each other make the six-petalled lotus symbol of the mystic Divine Embrace which completed the first act of creation.

The metaphysical concept is also personified in the image of the Divine Mother, who assumes many different names and forms, for every one of the divine beings, Devas or Devatās, projected

[1] Or, in a different connotation, fire and water respectively.

29

from the One Supreme and acting as controlling intelligences of different parts of the universal machine, has his Shakti, or female energy. Every personified icon has also its corresponding *yantra* and *mantra*, the *yantra* being the symbol of pure form and the *mantra* the symbol of pure sound emanating from the Divine Word which set the universe in motion.

Brahmā, the Creator, as Artist gives the divine Idea, setting out the limits of the universal plan ; Sarasvati, his Shakti, shapes it into things of beauty. As Musician He gives the time-beat of the universal rhythm ; Sarasvati sings the divine song, the Song of Life. The distinction is observed in Indian musical practice : the drummer who beats the time (*tāla*) is always a man. In the *rāgas* and *rāginis*, the melodic root-forms which are the terrestrial counterparts of the divine *mantras*, the difference of functions or qualities is also expressed in terms of sex.

¶ One of the few references to æsthetics so far discovered in Sanskrit literature—a dialogue between a king and his guru, or court chaplain, in the Vishnudharmottaram—emphasises the correspondence between music, dancing, and the art of the imager as different expressions of the universal rhythm. The student of the imager's art, which is closely connected with dancing (says the guru), should commence with learning the laws of singing, for all art is contained in the art

PLATE XII

SIVA AS DAKSHINAMURTI

(Southern India)

of song. The same thought is to be found in the imager's own motifs and technical rules. Siva, as Mahādeva the Supreme Being, dances the Dance of the Cosmic rhythm, beating the time-beat with his drum. Krishna, the divine flute-player, teaches the eternal law of pulsation in dancing with the Gopis. The *mudrās* and *hastas*, finger-play and arm movement, and the *vangus*, or bodily inflexions of Indian iconography, reproduce the gestures and movements of the deva-dāsi, the temple dancer. The Indian musician and the artist use the same word *tāla*, the former to indicate the time-beat, the latter for his unit of proportion, the length of the face, which is divided into twelve *angulas* and more minute fractions suggestive of the microtones of the musical scale. The musical *rāgas* and *rāginis* have their graphic and plastic counterparts in the imager's *dhyānas* and *lakhanas*, Sanskrit formu-laries laying down for his guidance firstly the spiritual meaning and secondly the physical attri-butes of the deity represented.

Ethics and æsthetics are thus perfectly syn-thesised in Indian art. The artist regards humanity, with all its spiritual, intellectual, and physical attributes, as the microcosm of the macrocosm. The Divine Pair, Man and Woman, representing the twin aspects of the Godhead, Purusha and Prakriti, Mind and Matter, symbolise the working of the universal æsthetic law, as it is imaged in the artist's mind. It is not the physical charms of the female form divine which are to captivate the worshipper—Indian art knows no Aphrodite or Diana—but the majesty and mystery of divine motherhood, expressed with wonderful sincerity of feeling and splendid craftsmanship in the image of Tārā, the Saviouress, one of the conceptions of Mahāyāna Buddhism (Plate XIII). The commanding pose, the jewelled tiara, and the right foot resting on the world-lotus proclaim her a queen of heaven. With the open right hand she bestows a gift upon the worshipper. In her left she holds a lotus flower : the colour of the flower signifies the special aspect of divinity displayed in the image. If it is white—without colour yet containing all colours—pure spirit is indicated. If it is red, the creative energy. Blue, the benign static power of the Maintainer of life, Vishnu, or his Mahāyānist counterpart, Avalokiteshvara. In this case the shape of the flower suggests the blue lotus.

In its austerity of outlook, simplicity of rhythm, and robust technique this image is typically Indian, of the classical school which had its great flowering time under the Gupta emperors, though this is several centuries later. We may compare with it a very graceful Tārā, Plate XV, of the still later Nepāli-Tibetan school, in hammered copper, gilt and elaborately jewelled, which shows how Chinese influence transformed the Indian

PLATE XIII

TĀRĀ

ideal. It is probably by the same hand as the image of Avalokiteshvara. (Plate IV.)

A beautiful image from Java, Plate XIV, later than the Indian Tārā described above, and more ornate and florid in its technique, shows the Divine Mother in her gracious aspect as Prajñā-pāramitā, the Spirit of Divine Wisdom, regarded as the Shakti of the Ādi-Buddha, the supreme deity of the Mahāyāna school. The body and the lower limbs have the rigid pose of the yogic trance, but the hands make the symbolic gestures (*mudrās*) of a spiritual teacher, and a book of the Law rests upon the lotus flower twined round her left arm.

It has been conjectured, says Dr. Vogel, that this image, while rendering the Buddhist ideal of Supreme Wisdom, is also intended as the post-humous statue of a Javanese queen, the consort of Rājasa, the first king of Singhasāri, *circa* A.D. 1222. In Java it was customary to raise temples over the ashes of deceased kings and queens, and to enshrine in them cult images bearing their likeness.[1]

All Indian images, Buddhist as well as Hindu, are given the attributes and insignia of royalty when they are meant to express the power of the Godhead in which the divine law, *dharma*, is embodied. God, as Power, is King or Queen—

[1] " The Influences of Indian Art " (India Society's publication), pp. 84–5.

1616a

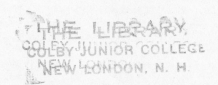

for the imager is allowed a certain latitude with regard to sex. God, as pure spirit, is the celibate monk or *muni*. The earthly monarch, who by virtue of his office is the defender of *dharma*, has always by his side his guru, or *purohita*, a disinterested spiritual adviser who is assumed to be an infallible interpreter of the Law and an expert in divine science. The Javanese temple builders were therefore only expressing the Indian sentiment that a dutiful king or queen was an incarnation of divinity and as such entitled to divine honours. An Indian king often took the name of his *Ishta-devata*, his patron deity.

The duality of the Godhead as Being and Power is not always imaged as two distinct persons, the god and goddess. Brahmanical philosophy insisted that, as these concepts were only the two aspects of the One, they must be combined in one icon. The Ardha-nāri image of Siva in the great temple of Elephanta, an androgynous figure, half-male and half-female, in which the sculptor attempted to render the metaphysical idea realistically, is an artistic fiasco, although the three-headed bust of the Trimūrti in the same temple is wonderfully impressive. The artistic difficulty is met quite simply and satisfactorily in the image of the Dancing Siva, Plate XXIV, by putting a man's ornament in one ear and a woman's ornament in the other.

The Indian imager deals with abstruse meta-

PLATE XIV

PRAJÑĀPĀRAMITĀ, FROM SINGHASĀRI, JAVA

(Ethnographic Museum, Leyden)

PLATE XV

TĀRĀ, TIBET OR NEPAL

(Calcutta Art Gallery)

physical ideas, which in the West are generally
held to be beyond the limitations of art, and
approaches them with so much reverence and
sincerity that he rarely falls into banality or
coarseness.

In the exquisite bas-relief of the two divinities
of the underworld, Plate XVI, the sculptor,
inspired by the romantic legends of the Indian
water-sprites, has succeeded in rendering the
mystic union of the Divine Pair with unaffected
poetic feeling and masterly design. Joined
together under the canopy of their extended
serpent-hoods, making a glory round their heads,
the goddess clings round the neck of her lord
with her right arm, holding a lotus flower to his
breast with her left, while he with both hands
encircles their two bodies with a wedding garland,
the sweeping curve of which makes rhythmic play
with the jewelled collars and the movement of the
arms. The subtle gradations of surface modelling, carried out to a delicate but not redundant
finish, enhance the striking beauty of the linear
design.

The Divine Power as god and goddess has
another form of activity besides the creative
one, exercised in the eternal conflict between
good and evil, the Devas and Asuras. This is
the constant theme of the Indian imager—Siva
crushing a dwarf demon under his foot (Plate
XXIV), or fighting the enemies of the gods

(Plate XXI) ; Vishnu in his Lion incarnation slaying the impious king Hiranya-kāçipu (Plate XXIII) ; Durgā destroying the buffalo-demon Mahisha (Plate XX) ; Manjusri armed with the sword of knowledge to destroy ignorance (Plate XVIII).

One of the many schools of Indian religious thought, the Shāktas, worship the divine Mother-Power as the supreme deity, under the name of Kālī, Devi, Mahā-Shaktī, and others. " She is the Great Queen (Mahārājnī) of Heaven and of yet higher worlds, of earth, and of the underworlds. To Her both Devas, Devis, and men give worship. Her feet are adored by even Brahmā, Vishnu, and Rudra."[1]

Shākta philosophy, says Sir John Woodroffe, in several respects gives an original presentment, both as regards doctrine and practice, of the great Vedantic theme of the One and Many. Shākta worship is perhaps the oldest of the many primitive cults which Vedantic philosophy assimilated and transformed, for in the remotest antiquity the goddess seems always to have taken precedence over the god, but its contributions to Indian art have not been great. Shākta ritual uses the symbolism of the yantra in preference to that of the icon, and most of the artistic conceptions of the Divine Mother have been appro-

[1] "The Indian Magna Mater," by Sir John Woodroffe, " Indian Art and Letters," vol. ii, No. 2.

PLATE XVI

A NĀGA AND NĀGINI

(Indian Museum, Calcutta)

priated by the other sects in which the Supreme Divinity is always God.

Kālī, as described in Shākta literature, is the personification of the Supreme Power which withdraws everything into Herself at the dissolution of the Universe. She stands naked in the dread cremation ground of space, where all worldly desires are burned away, dark as the Void in which the germ of all things reposed before the world began, dancing the Dance of universal destruction with dishevelled hair, lolling tongue, and with blood trickling from the corners of her mouth. A long string of skulls hangs round her neck, " the garland of letters," symbolising the universe of names and forms now being drawn into Her undivided Consciousness. Under her feet lies the prostrate corpse-like body of her husband, Siva. " He is white, because He is the illuminating (Prakēsha), transcendental aspect of Consciousness. He is inert, because the Changeless Aspect of the Supreme. In truth She and He are one and the same, being twin aspects of the One who is changelessness in and exists as change." [1] The devout Shākta worshipper who tries to penetrate behind the veil of illusion which envelops this dread aspect of Kālī, the Destroyer of Time, fixes his mind on the light and peace of spiritual liberation to which the Divine Mother leads her children.

[1] " Garland of Letters," by Sir John Woodroffe, pp. 221–2.

The Shākta artist, however, seems to have rarely succeeded in clothing the imagery of these transcendental ideas with dignity and dramatic power. At their best, images of Kālī are a variation of the Natārāja without its superb grace and beauty of design. At their worst, in modern images, a black doll devoid of all artistic feeling serves to symbolise the concept of the great Mother of Nature.

DHARMAPĀLA
(Batavian Museum, Java)

38]

Sword of
Knowledge

PLATE XVIII

MANJUSRI

(Calcutta Art Gallery)

CHAPTER IV

MYTHOLOGY AND METAPHYSICS

MYTHOLOGY, and the doctrine of re-incarnation which is fundamental to all Indian religious teaching, gave a more natural human interest to the metaphysical ideas which the temple sculptor and painter tried to express. The divine Buddha was incarnated as the Sakyan Prince whose life-story and previous births (*jātakas*) were carved or painted on every relic shrine for the edification of pilgrims. By followers of other sects Sakya Muni was regarded as one of the ten incarnations of Vishnu, among which were Rāma, the famous king of Ayodhya, whose adventures were told by every village story-teller, and Krishna, the divine Cowherd and hero of the Great War, who led the Pāndavas to victory. Siva, the Great God himself, lived in his icy cell on Mt. Kailāsa the usual life of an Indian Yogi, served by his other self, his devoted wife, Parvatī, King Himalaya's fair daughter, except when he was helping the other gods in their warfare with the Asuras and showed himself in all the majesty of the Godhead.

39

There was, therefore, no lack of subjects which the sculptor and painter might use for the decoration of temples, monasteries, kings' palaces, and more humble dwelling-places. But the icon which was the object of worship in the inner shrine of the temple stood in a category by itself, as a special symbol of the divine nature, and demanded the skill of the finest craftsmen. The legends of the Buddha's life on earth coloured the imager's conception of him as the Divine Yogi, and Buddhist art, before Mahāyāna doctrines reshaped it after its own cosmological notions, was so far in sympathy with the Gandhāran school that it never attempted the physiological impossibilities or abnormalities with which Hinduism deliberately invested the Divine Form. The typical Buddha image was in human shape, of a type familiar to every Indian, only made of a purer, finer substance than ordinary flesh and blood.

But orthodox Hindu teaching always held it to be irreverent and illogical to found artistic ideals of the Divine solely upon the contemplation of the human form. " The artist," says Sukracharya,[1] " should attain to images of the gods by

[1] Sukrachārya is the reputed author of an ancient Sanskrit work, " Sukra-nitisāra," or " The Elements of Polity by Sukrachārya." The fourth chapter, besides discoursing on politics, law, reformatory institutions, and the punishment of criminals, deals with arts and sciences, the building of castles, temples, bridges, and ships, the making and repairing of images, gardening, and the digging of wells, etc. It was translated into Tibetan in the seventh century A.D.

means of spiritual contemplation only. The spiritual vision is the best and truest standard for him. He should depend upon it and not at all upon the visible objects perceived by external senses. It is always commendable for the artist to draw the images of the Gods. To make human figures is bad, and even irreligious. It is far better to present the figure of a god, though it is not beautiful, than to reproduce a remarkably handsome human figure."

"Spiritual contemplation." Here is the key-note of Hindu art, as it was that of the art of Fra Angelico and other great Christian masters. The whole philosophy of Indian art is in these two words, and they explain a great deal that often seems incomprehensible and even offensive to Europeans.

While the Greeks made the perfect human body the highest ideal for an artist, there has been always in Indian thought a deep-rooted objection to anthropomorphic representations of the Divine. The Aryans in early Vedic times built no temples, and image-worship was not recognised in their higher ritual. The Hindu Sāstras hold that it is unlucky to have any representation of a human figure within the inner precincts of a temple. The substitution of a plain stone emblem of phallic origin for an anthropomorphic image in Saiva worship may be due to this feeling. The change appears to have taken place about the

5

time of the great Hindu reformer of the eighth century, Sankarāchārya, who regarded the Lingam as a symbol of the Eternal Unity, or of the " formless god." [1]

In the temple of Chidambaram in Southern India the Cause of all things is represented by space—an empty cell—showing a fine perception of the limitations of art ; for how can art, which is knowledge and expression, represent the Unknowable and Inexpressible ?

The Mosaic law declares, " Thou shalt not make to thyself any graven image or likeness of anything that is in heaven or earth." The Buddha forbade the decoration of monasteries with human figures. The Sunna, the law of Islam, likewise forbids the representation of animate nature in art.

The Buddhist creed originally was simply a rule of life founded on the precepts of right views, right resolves, right speech, right actions and

[1] The phallic symbol, though found in the Saiva temples of Java, does not appear to have been the principal object of adoration there, as it is now at Benares, the great centre of Saiva worship in India. From the number of statues of Siva found in Java we may conjecture that the worship of his image in human, or superhuman form, was also predominant in northern India, the birthplace of Saivism, before the time of Sankarāchārya, as it still is in the south. At the time of Hiuen Tsang's visit the principal object of worship at Benares was a statue of Siva, a hundred feet high, " grave and majestic, filling the spectator with awe, and seeming as it were alive." If the disuse of anthropomorphic images were only a consequence of the Muhammadan conquest it would have applied to the images of all other Hindu sects.

PLATE XIX

THE BUDDHIST TRIMŪRTI

(Calcutta Art Gallery)

living, right effort, right self-knowledge, and right meditation. Its ritual at first was purely symbolical and non-idolatrous, though the Buddha's followers in after times adopted the image of the Master, or rather that of his spiritualised Self, as an object of worship. For several centuries this spiritualised human type dominated the ideals of Buddhist art, but when orthodox Brahmanical influence began gradually to assert itself more and more strongly in Buddhism we find Indian artists attempting to differentiate the spiritual or divine type from the human by endowing the former with superhuman attributes, quite regardless of physiological possibilities or probabilities. Indian art has never produced a Phidias or Praxiteles, not because an Olympian Zeus or an Aphrodite of Cnidus was beyond its grasp, but because it deliberately chose imaginative rather than naturalistic ideals of the divine form.

The old Hebraic tradition, like the Greek, declared that God made man in His own image ; but the Hindu conception of the Cause of all things was of something much more vast and unapproachable—a vision too tremendous for human eyes to realise. In one of the most striking passages of the Bhagavad Gītā, Krishna reveals to Arjuna the nature of his Divinity. It has been finely rendered into English by Sister Nivedita thus : [1]

[1] " Cradle Tales of Hinduism," p. 215.

" I am the Soul, O Arjuna, seated in the heart of every being. I am the beginning, the middle, and the end of all things. Vishnu among the gods am I, among the lights I am the Sun. I am the mind among the Senses, the moon among the Stars. Amongst the waters, I am Ocean himself. Amongst trees, the Aswattha (Bo-tree) Tree am I ; amongst weapons the thunderbolt ; and Time amongst events. Of rivers I am the Ganges. Of created things I am the beginning, the middle, and the end. Time eternal am I, and the Ordainer, with face turned on every side ! Death that seizeth all, and the source of all that is to be. I am the splendour of those that are splendid. I am Victory, I am Exertion, I am the Goodness of the good. I am the Rod of those that chastise, and the Policy of them who seek victory. I am the Silence amongst things that are secret, and the Knowledge of those possessed of knowledge. That which is the seed of all things, I am That ! Supporting this entire universe with a portion only of My strength, I stand ! "

Arjuna begged of his divine Charioteer to show him his Eternal Self, his Universal Form ; but Krishna replied : " Thou art not able to look upon Me with this eye of thine. I will give thee an eye divine. See now My sovereign, mystic nature ! "

Then, when Arjuna looked, he saw a resplendent vision, filling all the space between earth and heaven, glowing as a mass of light in every region,

PLATE XX

DURGĀ SLAYING MAHISHA

(Ethnographic Museum, Leyden)

bright as the sun, and vast beyond all thought.
It was Something with innumerable arms and
faces turned everywhere, uniting in its body all
the gods, all men, and all created things. Even
with the supernatural power bestowed upon him
Arjuna was appalled by this wondrous trans-
figuration and begged of Krishna to resume his
milder " four-armed form." He received the
solemn warning :

> By favour, through my mystic form divine,
> Arjuna, thou My form supreme hast seen,
> Resplendent, Universal, Infinite,
> Primeval, seen before by none but thee.
> Yet not by Vedas, nor by sacrifice,
> By study, alms, good works or rites austere
> Can this My form be seen by mortal man,
> O Prince of Kurus ! but by thee alone !

Hindu philosophy thus clearly recognises the
impossibility of human art realising the form of
God. It therefore creates in Indian painting and
sculpture a symbolical representation of those,
milder, humanised, but still superhuman, divine
appearances which mortal eyes can bear to look
upon. A figure with three heads and four, six,
or eight arms seems to a European a barbaric
conception, though it is not less physiologically
impossible than the wings growing from the human
scapula in the European representation of angels—
an idea probably borrowed from the East. But
it is altogether foolish to condemn such artistic

allegories *a priori*, because they may not conform
to the canons of the classic art of Europe. All
art is suggestion and convention, and if Indian
artists by their conventions can suggest divine
attributes to Indian people with Indian culture,
they have fulfilled the purpose of their art. It
is the unfortunate tendency of modern European
education to reduce art to mere rules of logic or
technique, anatomy or perspective, style or
fashion, so that the creative faculty on which the
vitality of art depends is drowned in empty
formularies of no intellectual, moral, or æsthetic
value.

A bad craftsman certainly may make multiple
arms and heads appear clumsy and ridiculous,
but in the finest Indian images, such as Plates
XII, XVII, XXI, and XXIV, they are designed
with so much decorative feeling and articulated so
skilfully with the normal human body that they
appear as natural as the body of a Greek centaur
or faun. There are often intense imaginative
power and artistic skill in these Indian conceptions, as anyone who attempts to study them
without prejudice will realise. What tremendous
energy and divine fury are concentrated in the
bronze statuette of Dharmapāla (Plate XVII),
a manifestation of the Supreme Buddha as
Defender of the Faith, trampling underfoot the
enemies of religion! And what a suggestion of
majesty and restrained power there is in the

PLATE XXI

SIVA AS BHAIRAVA

(Elephanta)

Manjusri (Plate XVIII), the Bodhisattva representing creative science,[1] dispelling ignorance
with his uplifted sword of knowledge! This is
from a gilt copper statuette in the Calcutta Art
Gallery, which is interesting as a historical landmark, for the inscription on it in Nepalese shows
that it was made to commemorate the death of a
learned pandit and dedicated to a Nepalese
shrine in the year A.D. 1782.[2] It has all the fine
sentiment and decorative skill of the older work,
although the technique, especially in the modelling
of the lower limbs, is perfunctory and cannot
compare with the much finer execution of the
earlier Nepalese school from the same collection
illustrated in Plate XIX. This is a three-headed
and six-armed divinity cast in copper and gilt, probably representing the Buddhist Triad—Manjusri,
Avalokiteshvara (Padmapāni), and Vajrapāni,
corresponding to the Hindu Trimūrti, Brahma,
Vishnu, and Siva. The modelling and movement
of this little image are superb.

Hindu sculpture has produced a masterpiece
in the great stone alto-rilievo of Durgā slaying

[1] " Manjusri is the Buddhist analogue of the Hindu Brahmā, or
Vishvakarma. He is the great architect who constructs the man-
sions of the world by the supreme Ādi-Buddha's command, as
Padmapāni by his command creates all animate beings."—B.
Hodgson, " Languages, Literature, and Religions of Nepal," p. 43.

[2] The full inscription, translated, is as follows : " Blessing !
Hail, Khagamaju ! On the occasion of the death of Buddhacharya
Ratna Traya this image of Manjusri was made in the Samvat year
902, month of Kartika, 10th day of the waning moon. Bliss ! "

the demon Mahisha, found at Singhasāri, in Java,
now in the Ethnographic Museum, Leyden (Plate
XX). It belongs to the period of Brahmanical
ascendancy in Java, which lasted from about
A.D. 950 to 1500. The goddess is striding over
the prostrate carcass of the buffalo, in which
disguise Mahisha has concealed himself, and
seizing the real dwarf-like form of the demon, she
is preparing to deal him his deathblow. Judged
by any standard it is a wonderful work of art,
grandly composed, splendidly thorough in technique, expressing with extraordinary power and
concentrated passion the wrath and might of the
Supreme Beneficence roused to warfare with the
Spirit of Evil.

The student will find in this phase of Indian
imaginative art an intensity of feeling—a wonderful suggestion of elemental passion transcending
all the feeble emotions of humanity—a revelation
of powers of the Unseen which nothing in European art has ever approached, unless it be in the
creations of Michelangelo or in the music of
Wagner. But such qualities cannot be adequately
realised in isolated sculptures collected in
museums and art galleries ; to be fully appreciated
they must be seen in their proper environment
and in the atmosphere of the thought which
created them.

In the cave-temples of Elephanta, Ellora, and
Ajantā Indian sculptors played with chiaroscuro

PLATE XXII

RĀVANA UNDER KAILĀSA

(Ellora)

in great masses of living rock with the same feeling as the Gothic cathedral builders, or as Wagner played with tonal effects, hewing out on a colossal scale the grander contrasts of light and shade to give a fitting atmosphere of mystery and awe to the paintings and sculpture which told the endless legends of the Buddha or the fantastic myths of the Hindu Valhalla.

Though they cannot reproduce this atmosphere the three following plates (XXI to XXIII) will give some idea of the imaginative power and artistic skill of Indian sculptors in dealing with compositions of great dimensions. They are examples of the finest period of Hindu sculpture, from about the sixth to the eighth century A.D., when orthodox Hinduism in India had triumphed over Buddhism, and before Hinduism had succumbed to the Muhammadan invader. The art traditions, however, were a direct inheritance from Buddhism.

Plate XXI is a splendid fragment from the great temple of Elephanta of a colossal sculpture of Siva. It was mutilated by the Portuguese in the sixteenth century, but enough remains to show the noble composition and movement, and the broad but subtle modelling of the head, shoulders, and trunk, suggesting the etherealised divine body, with its broad shoulders, slim waist, smooth skin, and refined contours.

Plate XXII is from the wonderful Kailāsa

temple at Ellora, a monolithic idealised rendering of Siva's Himalayan hermitage, intended to suggest to the pilgrims that by the grace of Vishvakarma, the temple craftsman's patron deity, a replica of the Divine Yogi's heavenly cell had been put down for them at this sacred spot, so that they might be spared the long and perilous climb to the real Kailāsa.

The sculpture illustrates one of the weird legends of the strife between Rāvana, the ten-headed demon-king of Ceylon, and Rāma, the hero of the Rāmāyana. Rāvana, finding himself worsted in the fight with Rāma and his monkey allies, flies in his magic car to Kailāsa, and placing himself beneath the mountain, strives with all his demon's strength to lift it up, hoping to carry off Siva and the whole Hindu Olympus, and thus masterfully to compel the great god's aid against his mortal foe.

Rāvana is shown in the cavern he has made beneath Kailāsa, exerting terrific force in his effort to lift it up. The mountain quakes, and Parvati, Siva's wife, startled by the shock, clutches her husband's arm and cries out, " Some-one is moving the mountain ; we shall be over-thrown ! " Her maid is flying in alarm, but Siva, only raising one foot, presses down Kailāsa upon Rāvana's head and holds him fast.

The rest of the legend says that the wicked demon-king remained a prisoner for ten thousand years, until his grandfather, Pulastya, son of Brahmā, teaches him to propitiate Siva, and obtain pardon for his crimes by performing penances and becoming a devotee of the god.

The story is told with intense dramatic force and imagination in this great sculpture. The whole execution shows an extraordinary command of plastic technique, not only in the grouping and composition of line but in the powerful and subtle treatment of the varied gradations of relief. With the feeling of a Rembrandt for effects of chiaroscuro, the sculptor has concentrated masses of deep shadow and strong broken light upon the crouching, struggling figure of Rāvana, which throws into high relief all the horror of his demoniacal power. On the mountain-top where Siva sits enthroned, the serenity of his paradise— hardly disturbed by Parvati's sudden movement and the alarm of her handmaid—is finely suggested in quieter alternations and gradations of relief, softened by a veil of half-shade which falls over them from above.

The licence which the Indian artist allows himself, more especially in mythological scenes, of varying the proportions in figures of the same group, has been used here with great judgment and discretion. The two principal figures in high relief, the attendant deities on the right and left, and the crowds of lesser divinities and celestial beings, all play admirably their respective parts in the whole scheme. And the astonishing freedom with which this great sculpture is carved from the living rock, without any of the mechanical aids of the modern sculptor, makes it a splendid *tour de force*, quite apart from its higher artistic qualities.

Both at Ellora and Elephanta, as well as at Ajantā and other places, the sculptures, like the Greek statuettes of Tanagra, were carefully finished with a thin coating of the finest limeplaster, often as a preparation for colour and gilding—a process analogous to the *ganōsis*, or waxing, upon which Greek sculptors placed so high a value. At Ellora the whole of the exterior of the temple was given the effect of polished white marble, to suggest the glittering snow of the real Kailāsa. The interior of the *mandapam* was painted in fresco. This plaster finish has often perished by age, by ill-treatment, or exposure, but frequently it has been deliberately removed by amateur archæologists in their zeal for restoration. The process is still used by Indian sculptors and builders, though common whitewash, carelessly applied, is often substituted for it.

Plate XXIII is a fine fragment from the Das Avatāra cave at Ellora, the temple of Vishnu whose cult is the principal modern rival to that of Siva. This sculpture represents a myth connected with Vishnu's appearance on earth as the

NARASINGHA AND HIRANYA-KĀÇIPU

(Das Avatâra Cave at Ellora)

52]

man-lion, one of his ten incarnations. The story is told in the Vishnu-purāna. Hiranya-kāçipu, king of the Asuras and one of the doorkeepers of Vishnu's paradise, had obtained from Brahmā by severe penances the boon that he should not be slain by any created being. Inflated with pride, he then attempted to usurp the sovereignty of Vishnu, and ordered his son, Prahlāda, to offer him the worship due to the god. Prahlāda refused and braved all the wrath of his infuriated father. When Hiranya struck him he only thought on Vishnu, and the blows fell harmless. He was cast into the fire and was not burnt. With thoughts still fixed on the Preserver, he remained uninjured when elephants tried to trample him to death, and when thrown fettered into the sea a fish, at Vishnu's command, carried him safely ashore.

At last, as Prahlāda continued praying to Vishnu and proclaiming that He was everywhere and in everything, Hiranya tauntingly asked, " If that is so, why dost thou not show him to me ? "

Upon this Prahlāda arose and struck a column of the hall in which they stood, and behold, Vishnu issued forth in a Form which was half-man and half-lion, and tore the impious Asura king to pieces.

The sculptor has chosen the moment when the terrific apparition of the Man-lion rushes forth to seize Hiranya, who, taken unawares and with the mocking taunt still on his lips, makes a desperate effort to defend himself.

Any artist will appreciate the technical strength and imaginative power with which the subjects are treated in these sculptures. It would, however, be impossible to give an adequate impression of the great sculptured monuments of India within the compass of a single volume, even if sufficient material were available. But artistic research in India, though it has received a great impetus of late years, is still in its infancy. And even if the opportunities for artists were greater than they are there are some qualities in art which are almost impossible to explain.

No books or illustrations can give the haunting mystery of the Gothic cathedrals, or the subtle influence of the interior of St. Mark's at Venice. That only can be realised by seeing them with a mind and disposition for appreciation. Ruskin has truly said, " The arts, as regards teachableness, differ from the sciences in this, that their power is founded not only on facts which can be communicated, but on dispositions which require to be created." I can only hope in the illustrations I have selected to explain the motives and ideals, and to analyse the principles on which the master works of Indian fine art were based, leaving the rest to those who have the disposition and the opportunities for learning.

Apart from the wanton destruction by bigots and Philistines, and the destructive influences of a tropical climate, there is a special reason why masterpieces of fine art seem to be rare in India compared with their number in Europe. This must always seem to be the case in an art which is entirely creative and imaginative, instead of naturalistic. For while imagination is the supremest virtue of the artist, it is also the most rare. Works of the highest imaginative power have not been more rare in Indian art than they are in any country; but when a European fails in this highest poetic gift he finds a safe refuge in painstaking naturalism, which, to nine-tenths of the public, appeals more than imagination. The Indian artist is usually left without this resource of mediocrity, for the traditions of his art do not admit naturalism to be the highest aim, or even one of the principal aims—at least not in religious art. When he would play to the gallery he must fall back on extravagance and eccentricity, which excite the ridicule of the ignorant European critic. But more often he relies on his wonderful decorative instinct, and Indian art is always superbly decorative, even when it is wanting in the highest poetic qualities. It is only under European influence that it has fallen into the snare of commercialism, the last and worst vice of decadent intellectual powers.

Art will always be *caviare* to the vulgar, but

those who would really learn and understand it should begin with Indian art, for true Indian art is pure art stripped of the superfluities and vulgarities which delight the uneducated eye. Yet Indian art, being more subtle and recondite than the classic art of Europe, requires a higher degree of artistic understanding, and it rarely appeals to European dilettanti who, with a smattering of perspective, anatomy, rules of proportion and design, aspire to be art critics, amateur painters, sculptors, or architects, and these, unfortunately, have had the principal voice in deciding administrative questions which vitally affect India's artistic life. So the question whether Indian art is still a vital force, revealing India's spiritual self, seems to be less important than the question of taste—or whether from the European standpoint India's spiritual self should be allowed to reveal itself in art which the European and the Anglicised Indian do not appreciate or understand.

CHAPTER V

THE DANCE OF SIVA

WE have seen how Indian philosophy symbolises the Deity as pure form in the yantra ; as sound in the Divine Voice, represented by the mantras and by the rāgas and rāginis of Indian music ; again as pure thought, in the image of the Divine Yogi, and as thought-power in the person of the Divine Mother.

The Power of the Godhead is also conceived by the artist-philosopher in terms of motion or vibration. Siva is the Divine Dancer, who in 108 different movements interprets the mathematical law of the universe. The principal movement, known as the Nādānta dance, is represented with wonderful power in the famous bronze image of the Natārāja, the Lord of the Dance, now in the Madras Museum (Plate XXIV). Another form of the Dance, known as the Tāndavan, which is similar to Kālī's Dance of destruction, is shown among the sculptures of Elephanta and Ellora.[1]

[1] See " Ideals of Indian Art," by the author, Plates XXVIII and XXIX.

6   57

In the Nādānta dance Siva personifies the kinetic aspect of the Deity, or the Spiral Force of Yoga, regarded as the elemental force through which the universe is created, maintained, and eventually destroyed. In the image of the Divine Thinker, Siva (or the Dhyāni-Buddha) is only the static centre round which the moving cosmic forces revolve, as electrons revolve round the static centre of the atom.[1]

The symbolism of the spiral is universal in primitive art. It occurs frequently in Indian art and mythology in the form of the cosmic Serpent, Ananta, the Endless One, who is the couch and canopy of Vishnu, the Lord of Life. Also in the myth of the Churning of the Cosmic Ocean by the Devas and Asuras in order to obtain possession of the nectar of immortality. In this case Ananta, or Sesha, is used as the rope by which the churning stick is turned. The convolutions of the Sālāgrām stone and of the conch-shell, two of Vishnu's emblems, are other instances. In Vedic times Siva, under the name of Rudra, " The Roarer," [2] was the god of the whirlwind. But in this Natārāja image he is conceived mystically and metaphysically as the Divine Spirit, the Supreme Intelligence, dancing

---

[1] See " Serpent Power," by Sir John Woodroffe (Luzac), p. 69.

[2] Nādānta, derived from the Sanskrit root *nad*, to roar, is a metaphysical interpretation of the ancient Vedic concept. See Woodroffe's " Garland of Letters," p. 190.

PLATE XXIV

SIVA AS NATĀRĀJA

(Madras Central Museum)

Dancing Siva

in the human soul, removing sin and the effects of Karma. " They never see rebirths who behold this mystic Dance."

George Boole, the famous logician and mathematician, drew attention to a passage in the New Testament in which Christ uses the metaphor of the spiral in a similar mystic sense—a passage containing, he said, a psychological clue especially worth following up. " The wind bloweth where it listeth and thou hearest the sound thereof, but canst not tell whence it cometh or whither it goeth : so is everyone that is born of the Spirit " (St. John iii. 8). This, Boole pointed out, could not refer to wind travelling in a straight line, for of such a wind one knows whence it cometh and whither it goeth. In referring to the spiral track of the whirlwind Christ was thus using a familiar symbol embedded in the art of East and West from the earliest times.

According to the philosophy of Yoga, the cosmic spiral force known as Mahā-kundali, " the Great Coiled One," has also its seat in the human body ; for the latter, as the microcosm of the macrocosm, is said to have a series of psychic centres, corresponding to the spheres of the cosmic yantra, arranged one over the other from the base of the spine to the top of the brain. Each of these centres, in an ascending scale, represents different states of moral, intellectual, and psychic development. The highest, at the top of the brain, is called the Kailāsa of the body. By the practice and discipline of Yoga the adept is supposed to move the spiral force to gradually uncoil itself, like a serpent, from its central point at the base of the spine, until, when the Yoga is perfect, it reaches the Kailāsa of the body, and the state of ecstasy (*samādhi*) is produced in which the human consciousness is merged in the Universal and Siva reveals Himself. The power of the Yogi to achieve this result depends upon the purity of his own spiritual condition : he is following, mystically, or psychically, the arduous winding path by which the pilgrim ascends to Mahādeva's Himalayan hermitage.

The spiral is thus a symbol pregnant in meaning for Indian artists, as it represents the progress of the soul towards Nirvana, and the whole scheme of cosmic evolution. The Madras Museum Natārāja has been more discussed than any other figure in Indian iconography, but the most significant point conveyed by the main movement—that this is the Divine Yogi manifesting in His own body the spiral law of the cosmos, Mahā-kundali—has been hitherto unnoticed. Though this is not explicitly stated in the ritualistic texts, it is clearly shown in the varied movements of the limbs, in the rhythmic design of the contours, and even more emphatically in a very characteristic feature which makes this image unique in the Hindu pantheon—the wavy locks which are spread out as an aureole round Siva's head. The obvious mythological explanation is that the waves are symbolic of the sacred rivers which descend over Siva's head at Kailāsa, a small image of Gangā being enshrined in them. But this spreading out of the matted locks round the head, which is not seen in any other Siva image, could only occur in a whirling dance, like that of the modern dancing dervishes whose object is the same as that of the Yogi, to excite in the dancer a condition of psychic clairvoyance. This dance of Siva is still performed by the Devadāsis in the temples of Southern India, but in a much more stately and solemn tempo. Modern Saiva ritual does not, as a rule, recognise dancing for men ; but in Vedic India both men and Devas danced, and the appropriate dance for Siva in his Vedic aspect as Rudra, the storm-god, would be the dance of the whirlwind, as shown in the Natārāja image.

The mystic significance of the spiral, suggested by the combined movement of the body and limbs, would only be appreciated by the adept in Yoga. The more obvious symbolism of the minor gestures (*mudrās*) is explained in the Sanskrit ritualistic texts. The drum, shaped like an hour-glass and held in the upper right hand, beats the cosmic rhythm-sound representing the primary creative force and the intervals of

the beat the time-process. The flame held in
the corresponding left hand is the holy fire of
sacrifice. The other left hand stretched across
the body points to the uplifted foot of the Deity
as the refuge of salvation. The upraised hand
of the lower right arm, round which a cobra
is coiled, assures the devotee of divine protection;
the *torana*, or arch of flame surrounding the image,
is the Hall of the Universe in which Siva is
dancing.

The demon under Siva's right foot is Muyalaka,
the dark cloud of materialism in the Eternal
Ether (*Ākāśa*), which disappears in the sunshine
of the Divine Spirit. The popular mythological
explanation of the Dance, intended for those who
would not understand the occult meaning, is as
follows : Siva, disguised as an ordinary ascetic,
came to a forest hermitage where certain heretical
Rishis, his enemies, were assembled. He easily
confuted their arguments; they, in revenge, tried
to destroy him by black magic. First they
created a fierce tiger which sprang out of the
sacrificial fire. Siva seized it in its spring,
stripped off its skin with the nail of his little
finger, and wrapped it as a garment round his
loins. Then they created a venomous serpent.
Siva took it, wreathed it as a garland round his
neck, and began to dance. Whereupon another
evil shape, an ugly dwarf demon, rushed out of
the fire. Siva crushed it under his foot, broke

its back, and continued his triumphant dance, while all the Devas and all the Rishis assembled as witnesses of the Great Yogi's power.

Auguste Rodin has written [1] an impassioned appreciation of this splendid bronze from a craftsman's point of view, protesting against the narrow prejudice which has labelled this art as barbaric. The tribute from the great French master makes further comment almost super-fluous. It is wonderful how the movement of the Natārāja, in all its seeming *naïveté*, embodies the mystic idea of divine ecstasy. There is nothing in it of the mere animal gaiety of the Dancing Faun, nor any suggestion of the drunken frenzy of the Bacchanal. In its technical treatment the figure presents the same broad anatomical generalisation and the type of torso peculiar to the Indian divine ideal. No one who can appreci-ate the mastery of the structure of the human figure and the immense technical skill which the Hindu sculptor here shows can believe that it was from want of ability or knowledge that he has suppressed the smaller details of the muscular system. The Indian artist, as a rule, delights in elaborating detail when he thinks it necessary; but here, as in all his conceptions of Deity incar-nate, he has deliberately left out the human details which he thought inappropriate.

The image belongs to the Chola period, about

[1] " Ars Asiatica," vol. iii.

the tenth or eleventh century, when Indian art generally had lost the grand style of Gupta times. Compared with the best Elephanta sculptures, there is less impulsive energy in the whole conception, a certain suavity in the mode of expression —"puissamment doux," Rodin calls it. Another magnificent bronze image of the Natārāja,[1] first published by Mr. O. C. Gangoly, which stands in its original place in the great Tanjore temple, approaches nearer to the forcefulness of Elephanta in its energetic and passionate action. The power of its conception is enhanced by its size, for it is considerably larger than any other Natārāja known, the figure itself, excluding the pedestal and the *torana*, being nearly four feet in height. It is to be regretted that sufficient photographic material does not exist for a detailed comparison with the better-known images of the Madras Museum.

Though the temple imagers conform to fixed laws of proportion and design, laid down in the Silpā-śāstras, the rules are not so rigid as to suppress artistic individuality. There is a marked difference of movement and expression in different images : it is quite easy to distinguish the creative artist from the common craftsman who works only by rule. There are many examples of the Natārāja, good, bad, and indifferent, in the temples of Southern India and in public and private

[1] See "Handbook of Indian Art," by the author, Plate LXVA.

PLATE XXV

GANESHA DANCING
(Indian Museum, Calcutta)

collections. Some of the temple craftsmen of the present day show no mean artistry when they are called upon to represent the Lord of the Dance, though modern images cannot compare with the great masterpieces of Chola times.

Siva, as mentioned above, is said to dance in 108 different modes, though very few excepting the Nādānta dance are represented in temple images, probably because the spiral dance of Yoga sums up in itself the whole mechanism of the cosmos. Most of the other complementary modes of dancing are, however, carved as ornamentation on the gateway of the Natārāja temple at Chidambaram, with Sanskrit labels to distinguish them. Each dance may be said to symbolise some kinetic attribute of the Godhead ; a separate series of time-beats of the cosmic rhythm, like the musical rāgas ; or variations of the cosmic mathematical law. A series of serpentine dances is shown, representing spiral or gliding motion, one with a similar significance is named after a flash of lightning. The discus, or chakra, represents circular motion. Eight of them are based on the swastika, which probably is a symbol of the movement of the sun across the heavens. A leaping deer suggests the wave-line which in early Buddhist sculpture was used as a symbol of re-incarnation. A large number are difficult to identify, either from the sculptures or the texts, but the general idea seems obvious, that Siva,

the Divine Guru, teaches the geometrical law
of the cosmos by dancing.

Ganesha, or Ganapati, the elephant-headed
infant deity, which we may assume to be a
primitive tribal totem adopted by Brahmanism
as a son of Siva, is the popular guardian of house-
holds, remover of obstacles, patron of merchants,
authors, and schoolboys (for he is the scribe of the
gods), and god of common sense, who must be
invoked before every enterprise and mentioned
before any appeal to the Divine Spirit. This
quaint conception, which strikes the keynote of
Indian thought — the intimate relationship
between man and beast, is treated by Indian
sculptors in different moods, but always with
great sympathy and a full appreciation of its
artistic opportunities. In Plate XXV, a fine
sculpture from northern India, now in the Indian
Museum, Calcutta, Ganesha is shown in a spirit
of rollicking fun mimicking with entire self-
forgetfulness the tremendous cosmic dance of
Siva—a delightful blend of the grotesque with
the unconscious charm of infancy, and a masterly
study of sumptuous plastic harmonies designed
with the unfailing instinct of the Indian craftsman for decorative effect. The splendid example
of Indo-Javanese sculpture, Plate XXVI, now
in the Ethnographic Museum, Leyden, equally
rich and accomplished in technique, shows the
god in a graver mood with an air of elephantine

PLATE XXVI

GANESHA

(From Java)

sagacity, squatting complacently, in an awkward attempt to assume the ritualistic pose of " regal ease," on a row of human skulls which are a reminder of his descent from the Great Destroyer Siva. It is of the same school as the magnificent sculpture of Durgā slaying the Buffalo-demon, in the same collection (Plate XX), and possibly by the same artist.

CHAPTER VI

SCHOOLS OF SCULPTURE AND PAINTING

THOUGH it is impossible to classify Buddhist
and Hindu art into distinct schools on the basis
of dogmatic differences, Buddhism in practice,
if not in the essence of its teaching, was more
favourable to the development of the fine arts
than orthodox Hinduism, partly because for
some centuries it had predominant influence in
politics, and thus became more prolific in artistic
creation, and partly because Buddhism in its
origin was a protest against the tendency of
Brahmanical teaching to draw all men away from
the realities of life into the metaphysical atmosphere of spiritualistic speculation. On the other
hand it was Brahmanical thought which eventually transformed Buddhist ideals and gave art
in India its peculiar idiomatic expression.

The typical examples already shown are illus-
trative of the principal ideals of Indian art, but
do not give any clear indication of the separate
schools of sculpture which undoubtedly always
existed in India, though it has been commonly

assumed by European critics that the ritualistic and traditional character of Indian art imposed limitations upon it fatal to individual creative effort.

When Indian art was in its full vigour these limitations had no more restrictive effect upon artistic individuality than those which regulated the pre-Renaissance art of Europe. As in every great art epoch, certain traditional types were established, founded partly on sacerdotal prescription and partly on models created by the recognised masters of different schools.

So far as sculpture is concerned, the field is so wide and so much of it from an artistic point of view remains unexplored, that any attempt at a comprehensive classification of it according to schools must be more or less futile. Historical catalogues, arranged on an archæological basis, often without sufficient artistic discrimination, have little value as history and are often misleading as art. The European method of artistic exegesis, applied to India, will only provide more material for museums, the hobbies of the collector and for dealers in antiquities.

For real lovers of art it must always seem more important, before classifying Indian art according to schools and epochs after the method of the European historian, to realise that India has an unbroken artistic tradition going back for thousands of years. The discovery of a living Indian artist or craftsman, learned in the Silpā-śāstras and connected by a long line of ancestors with the most famous artists and craftsmen of antiquity, gives hope of keeping the springs of Indian craftsmanship flowing and an opportunity of historical study which is altogether denied to European art critics, even to those who search in our English villages for the last vestiges of traditional folk-music and art.

The fact, alluded to by Mr. O. C. Gangoly,[1] that in a village of the Tanjore District there exists at the present day a colony of temple imagers descended from the great school of Chola craftsmen who built, carved, and furnished the famous temple of Tanjore, brings the creators of the Natārāja to life and makes Indian art a reality instead of an academic pose. If it were only realised as such, it would be as significant a fact for India as the discovery of skilled English craftsmen descended from the builders of Westminster Abbey or Wells Cathedral would be for Mr. Stanley Baldwin.[2]

To bring about a real renaissance of art in India, the problem which must be solved is to find work and greater opportunities for the unemployed, or partially employed, artists and

[1] " South Indian Bronzes," pp. 26–7.

[2] The Prime Minister in an appeal for the preservation of old English cottages says that " we have to see if we cannot once again tap the springs of craftsmanship which have not flowed in this country for so long."

craftsmen who form India's own traditional
school of art, not to establish more schools
of a modern European type to keep them unemployed. But few of India's political mentors
seem inclined to make use of the opportunities
they now have of preventing any further wastage
of India's artistic resources, or to realise that a
vital art tradition once lost is lost for centuries,
and can hardly ever be revived. It cannot be
taught by schools, exhibitions, or museums, or
recovered by the fulfilment of political hopes and
ambitions.

For some years the Archæological Survey,
under the direction of Sir John Marshall, became
the best craft school in India by giving employment to many skilful sculptors in restoring the
famous monuments their ancestors had built.
But since that work was completed many of them
have been constrained to go on educating their
children for clerical or other occupations, as the
present public works system gives them no
opportunity for practising their own hereditary
crafts. One of the most interesting of the old
schools of sculpture thus helped by the Archæological Department is that of Orissa, represented
by the splendid temple of Kanārak and by some
fine modern buildings at Puri and elsewhere.[1]
Because, like the Hindu schools of Southern

[1] See " Indian Architecture," by the author, Plates CXXVII–
VIII.

India, it remained outside the influence of Islam, which emasculated most of the sculpture of the North, it still retains much of its pristine virility and imagination, though the school is fast dying out from lack of recognition.

If the springs of Indian craftsmanship, which have flowed spontaneously for ages, must always be harnessed to Western machinery, driven by European art-mechanics, the inevitable consequence is that they will sooner or later be pumped as dry as similar English springs have been made by the same mechanical process. Indians who care anything for art must, above all things, prevent the mechanising of their traditional schools of craftsmanship. It means not only permanent economic loss but that sterilisation of the creative faculties which has been manifested in the building of New Delhi. Nearly a century after the Anglicisation of Indian education began, departmentalism can discover no Indian with creative powers to build or adorn the Indian capital.

Under the guidance of Dr. Abanindra Nath Tagore, C.I.E., the leader of the new Calcutta School of painting, one family of the traditional school of Orissa is now working at Calcutta. The charming little panel, entitled "The Gardener's Daughter," Plate XXVII, by Shidhartha Mahāpatra, a happy blend of the new tradition with the old, shows what may be done by sympathetic

PLATE XXVII

THE GARDENER'S DAUGHTER, BY SHIDHARTHA MAHĀPATRA

(Modern Orissa School)

and wise encouragement of India's own art, which suffers more from the ban put upon it by Europe than from the iconoclasm of Islam.

A complete survey of the traditional schools of art and craft still existing in India, especially of those which have not been debased by Western commerce, would be of great value, though the remarkable evidence of the vitality of Indian craftsmanship collected in the Report on modern Indian Architecture, 1913,[1] has not persuaded the Public Works Department to revise its devastating methods in art.

The traditional canons of Indian art and craft are preserved in the Silpā-śāstras and other works, but Sanskrit literature makes very little reference to the schools of sculpture and painting attached to the ancient universities and other religious foundations in India. The most circumstantial information regarding the Indian schools of fine art, previous to Mogul times, is that given by Tāranath, a Tibetan Lama, who wrote a history of Buddhism in A.D. 1608. The last chapter, relating to sculpture and painting, has been translated by Mr. W. T. Heeley, I.C.S., in the "Indian Antiquary," vol. iv, p. 101. It gives many important landmarks in Indian art history.

" In former days," he writes, " human masters who were endowed with miraculous powers pro-

---

[1] Government Press, Allahabad.

duced astonishing works of art. It is expressly
stated in the Vinaya-āgama and other works
that the wall-paintings, etc., of those masters
were such as to deceive by the likeness to the
actual things depicted. For some centuries after
the departure of the Teacher many such masters
flourished. After they had ceased to flourish,
many masters appeared who were gods in human
form ; these erected the eight wonderful chaityas
of Magadha—the Mahābodhi, Manjusri-dun-
dhūbh-ishvara, etc. [the relic shrines marking
the chief sacred places of Buddhism], and many
other objects."

This refers to a period of which no known
artistic traces exist. There are other references to
picture-halls and sculptured images in the Mahābhārata, the Rāmāyana, and in the early Buddhist
records, but Indian architecture at that time
was almost entirely wooden ; the pictures, which
were mostly fresco paintings on a foundation
probably of wood or of unburnt clay, have entirely
disappeared together with the buildings. Tāranath only briefly refers to the important monuments of the great Buddhist Emperor Asoka,
circ. 274–237 B.C., some of which, such as those
at Bhārhut and Sānchī, still exist :

" In the time of King Asoka, Yaksha artisans
[a race of demigods or supernatural beings]
erected the chaityas of the eight great places,
the inner enclosure of the Vajrāsana, etc."

The Vajrāsana, " the diamond-throne," or the place under the bodhi-tree at Gāyā where the Buddha won enlightenment, was enclosed by a sculptured stone railing by Asoka. Part of this still exists.

" In the days of Nāgārjuna," continues Tāranath, bringing us down to about A.D. 150, " many works were performed by Nāga artisans. Thus the works of the Yakshas and Nāgas for many years deceived by their reality. When in process of time all this ceased to be, it seemed as if the knowledge of art had vanished from among men." The principal works of this epoch now existing are the early paintings of the Ajantā caves, the sculptured rail of Amarāvatī and some of the Gandhāra sculptures. " Then," says our historian, " for a long course of years appeared many artistic efforts, brought to light by the striving of individual genius, but no fixed school or succession of artists." After this rather vague and legendary account the Lama gives us some more precise details :

" Later, in the days of Buddha-paksha [the identity of this monarch is uncertain] the sculpture and painting of the artist Bimbasāra were especially wonderful, and resembled those early works of the gods. The number of his followers was exceedingly great, and, as he was born in Magadha, the artists of his school were called Madhyadesha artists. In the time of King Shīla there lived an especially skilful delineator of the gods born in Marwār, named Shringadhara : he left left behind him paintings and other master-pieces like those produced by the Yakshas. Those who followed his lead were called the old Western School."

The King Shīla referred to is probably the celebrated Harsha Vardhana Sīladitya (606–647), an account of whose empire is given in the narra-tive of Hiuen Tsang's pilgrimage. The finest of the paintings and sculptures of Ajantā may thus be attributed to this " Old Western " School.

" In the time of Kings Devapāla and Shrimant Sharmapāla there lived in Varendra (northern Bengal) an exceedingly skilful artist named Dhimān, whose son was Bhitpālo ; both of these produced many works in cast-metal, as well as sculptures and paintings, which resembled the works of the Nāgas. The father and son gave rise to distinct schools ; as the son lived in Bengal, the cast images of the gods produced by their followers were usually called gods of the Eastern style, whatever might be the birthplace of the actual designers. In painting the followers of the father were called the Eastern School ; those of the son, as they were most numerous in Ma-gadha, were called followers of the Madhyadesha School of painting. So in Nepāl the earlier schools of art resembled the Old Western School ; but in the course of time a peculiar Nepalese School was formed which in painting and casting resembled rather the Eastern types ; the latest artists have no special character."

The King Devapāla was the third of the Pāla dynasty of Bengal, and reigned about the middle of the ninth century.[1] Further research among the sculptures scattered about Bihar and Orissa might lead to the identification of Dhimān's and Bhitpālo's work. It is interesting to find that there was a school of painting and metal-work in Nepāl founded on the work of these masters, for the fine copper-gilt image of the Trimūrti (Plate XIX), and other examples of old Nepalese art, collected by the author for the Calcutta Art Gallery, may give an indication of their style. Tāranath proceeds to give some information regarding the Kashmir School :

" In Kashmir, too, there were in former times followers of the Old Western School of Madhya-desha ; later on a certain Hasurāya founded a new school of painting and sculpture, which is called the Kashmir School."

This interesting sketch of Indian art-history concludes with some remarks on the comparative influence of Buddhism, Muhammadanism, and orthodox Hinduism on art-development :

" Wherever Buddhism prevailed skilful religious artists were found, while wherever the Mlechchas

[1] Chronology of India," by C. Mabel Duff, p. 298.

(Muhammadans) ruled they disappeared. Where, again, the Tirthya doctrines (Orthodox Hinduism) prevailed, unskilful artists came to the front. Although in Pakam (Burma) and the southern countries the making of images is still going on, no specimens of their works appear to have reached Tibet. In the South three artists have had many followers : Jaya, Parojaya, and Vijaya."

Tāranath's allusion to the inferiority of the Hindu artists points perhaps to some of the esoteric influences in later Hinduism which have contributed to the neglect and contempt into which Indian fine art, especially sculpture, has fallen. It is probable that Sankarāchārya, the great Hindu reformer and apostle of the Vedānta, who lived about the ninth century, was, if not an iconoclast, like the followers of Islam, as much opposed in principle to image-worship as the Early Vedic philosophers, though tolerating it as a spiritual help for the ignorant masses. Sankarāchārya himself used geometric symbolism in his *sādhana* : the *yantra* called the Śrīchakra, said to have been used by him, is preserved in the famous Srīngeri Math he founded in Southern India.

Obviously the Vedantic doctrine of Māyā, which treats all Nature as illusion, might, if pushed to extremes, cut away the ground of all artistic creation just as the intense mental concentration which is the foundation of the Yoga School of philosophy might eventually lead to absolute quietism and intellectual sterility. These two tendencies may, therefore, have had some influence on the decadence of fine art in India.

In the days of Hindu political supremacy the manifold activities of a self-supporting and vigorous national life would tend to stimulate the creative powers of thought and counteract the depressing influence of a doctrine which led to a kind of intellectual nihilism, as far as sense-perception is concerned. But when these activities became subject to the tutelage of a foreign domination this stimulus ceased to be effective. Intellectual Hinduism gave itself up to its mystic reveries and ceased to interest itself in original artistic production.

Deprived on the one hand of the intellectual stimulus which gave it life, and, on the other, of the physical stimulus of state patronage, promoting a natural and healthy activity, it is not surprising that much of the Hindu sculpture of the present day has become a stereotyped repetition of conventional forms in which the highest poetic qualities of a " fine " art are generally lacking.

But this very conventionalism and stereotyped tradition have nevertheless been the means of preserving artistic qualities which raise some modern Indian architectural sculpture far above the level of what Europeans and English-educated Indians perversely substitute for it.

CHAPTER VII

THE HUMAN IDEAL AND THE SCULPTURES OF BHĀRHUT, SĀNCHĪ, AND AMARĀVATĪ

WE will now proceed to make acquaintance with a phase of Indian religious art which will appeal to most Europeans more than the study of oriental iconography, for it brings us down from the transcendental heights of philosophic Hinduism to the plane of our common humanity.

It is necessary, however, to bear in mind that though it might be supposed that in rendering the ordinary human form and events of human existence Indian art is exactly in the same plane of thought as European, there is nevertheless a wide difference between them. Greek and Italian art would bring the gods to earth and make them the most beautiful of men ; Indian art raises men up to heaven and makes them even as the gods. And until the fine arts were kept quite apart from religion, as in the Mogul period, the types of divine beauty established by artistic and ritualistic tradition profoundly influenced the artist's outlook upon life and the nature he saw around him.

The ideal of manly beauty he set before himself was not represented by a Rajput warrior, but by the divine Buddha, Krishna, or Siva. His idea of female beauty was not seen in the fairest of Indian women, but in Parvati, or in the heavenly Apsaras. Before, then, we begin to assume that Indian sculptors never attained to the same degree of technical achievement as Praxiteles or Michelangelo, we must always clearly understand how far it is possible to draw any comparison between them ; and except in their mutual reverence for the beauties of nature, and in the important part which art took in national life and education, there are not many points of analogy in the spirit of classic art and Indian.

In an age when reading and writing are rare accomplishments, the arts of painting and sculpture play a part in national life and education hardly to be realised nowadays. In the great epoch of Indian art which we are reviewing, art, religion, and education had no existence apart from each other as they have in this age of specialisation and materialism. They were similar and interchangeable forms and expressions of national thought and culture. The Buddhist monks were often themselves practising artists, and like the Christian monks of the Middle Ages they used the arts, not for vulgar amusement and distraction, but as instruments for the spiritual and intellectual improvement of the people.

And, like all true artists, they were keen observers and lovers of Nature. In choosing the places for their retreats, they always had the keenest eye for the beauties of hill and plain, mountain, forest, river, and sea. Dr. Burgess thus describes the prospect from the Elephanta Caves, the sculptures of which we have already discussed.

" The view from the front of the cave is one of exceeding beauty, commanding the fine bay between Elephanta, Bombay, and the mainland. From the grey dawn of morning till the shades of night close upon it, whether crowded with the white sails of hundreds of fishing craft, or only marked here and there with one or two passenger boats, and perhaps a small steamer, it is an ever fresh and varying scene of beauty. And a few steps from the porch will lead the visitor to the site of an old *bangalá* which commands the prospect to the south-west of Bombay and its splendid harbour, with Butcher Island in the foreground. Any true lover of Nature will feel himself amply rewarded by the magnificent views to be here enjoyed."

But beauty, for them, was for religion and love, not for idle pleasure ; they had the artistic insight which sees beneath and beyond the external facts and beauties of Nature. They always sought for and found—

Tongues in trees, books in the running brooks,
Sermons in stones, and good (God) in every thing.

The alternative reading of Shakespeare's text would make the philosophic Duke express perfectly the Eastern outlook upon nature. Mr. J. Griffiths, in noticing the wonderful position of the Ajantā Cave-temples, says :

" All the forces of Nature are considered by devout Buddhists as expressions and symbols of the faith. For the vulgar, the waterfall or the wind turns the mechanical prayer-wheel, but to those devoted to meditation and the cultivation of a higher life, the mere sound of running water, the rustle of the leaves as the wind plays through them, the movement of the clouds in the sky, and the manifold life and activity of the creatures of the jungle, are so many hymns of praise to the great harmonious law enunciated by the life of Buddha." [1]

The people themselves shared fully in the feeling of their spiritual leaders. To take the pilgrim's staff in hand and leave the worldly life, to be one with Nature in all her moods, was the supreme desire of every devout Buddhist or Hindu, whatever his sect might be. The pious Buddhist

[1] " Ajantā Caves," Introd., p. 1.

would set out to follow, step by step, the Master's
life on earth, from his birthplace in the Lumbini
garden to the final accomplishment of Pari-
Nirvāna at Kusināra. And, as the great story
was told again and again round the camp-fires at
night, the teeming life of the jungle round about
seemed to become part of it, and wondrous
legends grew of the jātakas, the Master's pre-
existences in the form of bird or beast, preparing
by many an act of devotion and self-sacrifice to
show the way of release for suffering humanity.

And then, as now, Siva's followers climbed the
winding pathway up the steep Himalayan slopes,
through a paradise of tree and flower, above the
dark forests of mighty deodar, to the region of
cloud and mist and eternal ice and snow ; gazing
there with awe on the shining glories of the silver
mountain where the great god sat in sublime
meditation.

Others would explore the country made sacred
in national song and legend ; they would tread
the sacred hill of Chitrakuta, and track the course
of Rāma's and Sītā's wanderings by the banks of
the Godavari and in the forests of the Deccan ;
roam over the battlefields of the heroes of the
Mahābhārata, and the scenes of Krishna's adventures and amours in the pastures of Brindaban.

And wherever the pilgrims went, and whatever
might be their creed, the gods were with them
always. They felt their presence in the countless

denizens, seen and unseen, of forest, field, or
flood. They heard them in the many voices of
the jungle ; in the winds which swept through
the forest trees, and in the waters which poured
down from their heaven-built Himalayan throne.
They knew their power and beauty by the rising
and setting of the sun ; by the radiant light and
heat of midday ; by the glories of the Eastern
moonlit nights ; by the majestic gathering of
the monsoon clouds ; by the fury of the cyclone,
the lightning flash and thunder, and the cheerful
dripping of the life-giving rain. From this devout
communion with Nature in all the marvellous
diversity of her tropical moods, came the inspiration of an art possessing a richness of imagery
and wealth of elaboration which seem bewilder-
ing and annoying to our dull Northern ways of
thinking.

Their art was glowing with spontaneous warmth
and fantasy, like the Nature which inspired it.
Yet it was not based upon a sensual Nature-
worship, like Hellenic art, but upon Nature
regarded as the manifestation of one great Universal Law. It was less coldly reasoned than
the art of Greece, but far more spiritual ; for
the poets and philosophers of a highly intellectual
age joined in using this jungle-lore which clung
round national history and popular beliefs as a
framework for moral and spiritual instruction,
inculcating by poetry, fable, and allegory the

supreme law of life which the Buddha preached and the eternal truth of the immanence of God.

The schools of art were not only the courts and palaces of kings, or offices of state, but the monasteries and the sacred shrines at which the pilgrims paid their devotions. The early history of this art and architecture belongs to a period when, the greater part of the country being covered by primeval forests, the most convenient material for building and sculpture was wood. But though in this perishable material no monuments of this earliest period actually survive, we can gather a clear idea of the style from the monuments of Asoka's time, in which all the forms of the ancient wooden construction are reproduced, and from the representations of buildings given at Bhārhut, Sānchī, and elsewhere. The modern wooden architecture of the sub-Himalayan countries, like Nepāl, and that of Burma, has many affinities with it.

It is not, however, the purpose of this book to give a history of Indian fine art, but rather to show the highest development of it at a time when the monasteries and sacred shrines had become great national sculpture and picture galleries ; and when, in the course of many centuries, the traditions of Indian art-practice had become perfected into a science which was afterwards reduced to writing and recorded in the literature of Indian ritual and religion. Modern

" educated " Indians, to their shame be it said, are mostly ignorant of or indifferent to this great science, the traditions of which are kept alive by the artistic castes of the present day ; though they are fast being crushed under the vandal heel of what we miscall civilisation, just as the traditions of the medieval artists and craftsmen have been extinguished by a barbarous and godless commercialism.

The practice of circumambulating a sacred shrine or place, one of the oldest of religious observances, gave rise to the decoration of the pilgrim's procession paths with painted and sculptured representations of sacred symbols and images, or illustrations of legendary or historical events. The painted decorations were generally the work of monks or of craftsmen supported by the donations of pilgrims ; the sculptures and images in the precious metals were often the gift of kings or other wealthy patrons.

The sculptured stone rails which enclosed the procession paths at Bhārhut, Sānchī, and Amarāvatī have been minutely described and illustrated in archæological works ; and as apart from their decorative beauty they do not represent the highest type of Indian sculpture, it is unnecessary to enter into detailed critical examination of them. Artistically they are extremely interesting because they illustrate the development of Indian sculpture from the time of Asoka (c. 274–237

B.C.), to whose reign the Bhārhut rail is attributed, down to about A.D. 170, the supposed date of the later Amarāvatī sculptures.

Obviously the construction of these rails is borrowed from wooden prototypes; but it is not only in constructional forms that they give indirect evidence of the ancient crafts of India, which are frequently alluded to in the Rāmāyana and Mahābhārata. The whole technique of the sculpture is a curious rendering in stone of the craftsmanship of wood-carvers, metal-workers, and painters, and as nothing similar to it is to be found in the sculpture of other countries, it will be interesting to inquire how this peculiar style originated.

Before the time of Asoka the principal artistic crafts of India, exclusive of weaving, were those of painting, wood-carving, and metal-work. The two former were no doubt practised in the Buddhist monasteries of Northern India, as they are now in Nepāl and Tibet. It must not be supposed that the mason's and stone-carver's art was unknown; but only that, as in all countries where wood is cheap and plentiful, the latter material was generally preferred for structural and decorative purposes; and, therefore, the wood-carvers greatly exceeded in number the craftsmen who worked in stone.

When Asoka succeeded to an empire greater than India had ever known before, and settled

down as a devout Buddhist to cultivate the arts
of peace, he employed the energies of his subjects
in constructing a vast number of monuments
and offices for the new state religion and many
magnificent public works ; and, as he desired
them to endure for ever, he made as many as
possible of brick and stone.

" Asoka," says Dr. Vincent Smith, " was a
great builder, and so deep was the impression
made on the popular imagination by the extent
and magnificence of his architectural works that
legend credited him with the creation of 84,000
stūpas, or sacred cupolas, within the space of
three years. When Fa-hien, the Chinese pilgrim,
visited Pātaliputra, the capital, at the beginning
of the fifth century A.D., in the reign of Chandra-
gupta Vikramāditya, the palace of Asoka was
still standing, and was deemed to have been
wrought by supernatural agency.
    " ' The royal palace and walls in the midst
of the city which exist now as of old, were all
made by the spirits which he employed, and
which piled up the stones, reared the walls and
gates, and executed the elegant carving and
inlaid sculpture work in a way which no human
hands of this world could accomplish.' "—*Early
History of India*, p. 144.

This extraordinary activity in building must
have created a demand for skilled masons and
sculptors much greater than India could supply ;

8

and just as in later times Shah Jahān brought
masons from Samarkand, Shiraz, and Baghdad
to assist in building the Tāj, so doubtless Asoka
imported numbers of skilled craftsmen from the
great cities of western Asia. We can still recognise their handiwork in the magnificent monolithic pillars, some of which are fifty feet in height
and about fifty tons in weight, wherewith Asoka
marked many of the sacred places of Buddhism.
The finest of these, unearthed at Sarnāth on the
spot where the Buddha preached his first sermon,
is a perfect specimen of the stone-mason's and
carver's art. The design is a Græco-Persian
rendering of the Indian world-pillar, shown in all
the buildings represented at Bhārhut and Sānchī.

The chief direction of all these works would
have remained in Indian hands, and the great
majority of the craftsmen must have been Indian
also, and therefore more accustomed to work in
wood, ivory, and metal than in stone. The wood-
carvers found in the red sandstone which abounds
in northern India an excellent material, which
could be worked with practically the same tools
as they had always used : there was no necessity
for them to alter their usual technique. Fergusson thought that the surprising degree of technical
skill shown in the Bhārhut sculptures proved that
stone must have been a material perfectly familiar
to the craftsmen who executed them, and that
their skill in lithic work must have been acquired

by centuries of practice as stone-carvers ; but on technical grounds it is not necessary to assume this. Even now there is very little difference in the tools used in India for decorative purposes by wood, stone, and metal workers, and technical skill acquired in one material could easily be transferred to another. The technique of the Bhārhut reliefs suggests that they were the work of skilled wood-carvers attempting for the first time to use stone. This would explain why the sculpture of the early stone monuments of India shows a much higher degree of technical perfection than is found in the first attempts at stone-carving of a primitive state of art-culture. The sculptors are not tyros in craftsmanship, but skilled wood or ivory carvers, or sometimes metal-workers.

Asoka was by principle averse from warfare, and India, under the greater part of his rule, enjoyed a profound peace, through the suppression of the rivalry and jealousy of the numerous petty states, then consolidated into one great empire. There was, therefore, less occupation for those who manufactured and ornamented weapons of war, but a great demand for skilled craftsmen in decorating the sacred shrines of Buddhism. The artist-monks also, now that Buddhism was the state religion, under the patronage of a powerful sovereign, were not satisfied with humble stūpas and monasteries of brick and clay decorated with fresco paintings on plaster ; they faced them with stone, and made painted *rilievos* instead of frescoes.

These circumstances explain the peculiar characteristics of the Bhārhut, Sānchī, and Amarāvatī sculptures. So vast was the labour bestowed on the decoration of the great Buddhist monuments that each became a permanent art centre and created a school of its own. The technical traditions were handed on from one generation of craftsmen to another, and so we find that even centuries afterwards when they were dealing with the hard limestone of Amarāvatī, they still reproduced in stone the artistic processes of the days of Asoka. Only in Western India, and some other localities, where Asoka's zeal for the Buddhist faith led to the carving of temples and monasteries out of the living rock, the craftsmen were forced to modify their methods, and other schools were created, with a perfectly lithic style of technique which culminated in the magnificent sculptures of Elephanta and Ellora already illustrated.

The Bhārhut rail is, according to Fergusson, the most interesting monument in India from an historical point of view. It is especially important for the study of Indian sculpture, because it shows the degree of technical development the fine arts in India had reached before India came in contact with the Græco-Roman art of Gan-

dhāra, before the Indian artistic ideal was perfected, and before Indian artistic philosophy had
been differentiated from that of classical Europe.
Fergusson says :

" It cannot be too strongly insisted that the
art here displayed is purely indigenous. There
is absolutely no trace of Egyptian influence ; it
is, indeed, in every detail antagonistic to that
art ; nor can it be affirmed that anything here
could have been borrowed directly from Babylonia or Assyria. The capitals of the pillars
do resemble somewhat those of Persepolis, and
the honey-suckle ornaments point in the same
direction ; but barring that, the art, especially
the figure sculpture belonging to the rail, seems
an art elaborated on the spot by Indians and by
Indians only." [1]

Fergusson's judgment in this matter, though
disputed by some archæologists, seems to me to be
perfectly sound. We must establish our theories
on the style as a whole, taking into consideration
the esoteric elements, not the external accretions,
as those which determine the character and
origin of it. The ordinary archæological method
is rather like trying to ascertain the nature and
growth of an oyster by analysing the crust
outside its shell, ignoring the living organism,
and perhaps a pearl, within.

The Bhārhut sculptures also show the interest-

[1] " History of Indian Architecture," p. 89.

ing fact that in Asoka's time the worship of the person of the Buddha was not a part of Buddhist ritual. "Everything is Buddhist, but it is Buddhism without Buddha. He nowhere appears either as a heavenly person to be worshipped, or even as an ascetic." The objects which attract the reverent homage of both men and beasts are the symbols of the faith; the sacred footprints, the bodhi-tree in which the Presence dwelt, but not the Presence itself. Much of the figure-sculpture at Bhārhut is very primitive, but there are some which prove that, several centuries before the Gandhāran School had developed its ideal, Indian sculptors without foreign tuition had achieved no mean skill in rendering the human form.

The figure called Sudarsanā-Yakshini (Plate XXVIII) is one of the best of a series of semi-divine beings which appear as guardians at the four entrances, on the upright supports of the rail. The two most obvious points to be noticed in it are, first, that the technique is entirely that of a wood-carver; and, second, that the treatment is frankly naturalistic. There is no attempt to idealise; no indication of the abnormally narrow waist or of the complete suppression of the muscular details which are characteristic of all later Indian sculpture. Here we have "the shoulders loaded with broad chains, the arms and legs covered with metal rings, and

PLATE XXVIII

RELIEF FROM BHÁRHUT

(The Sudarsaná-Yakshiní)

the body encircled with richly linked girdles,"
which, according to Professor Grünwedel, prevented Indian sculptors from producing an ana-
tomically correct form. Yet the main anatomical
facts are remarkably well given, especially the
difficult movement of the hips. In fact, it is very
surprising that in this, one of the earliest known
monuments of Indian art, we find such a high
degree of technical achievement and such careful
study of anatomy.

If we accept the conclusion that the Indian
artistic ideal is a feeble attempt to imitate Gandhāran models, or those of Græco-Roman art, we
must assume that many centuries later than these
Bhārhut sculptures, when every branch of art had
progressed and India was the acknowledged
head of the scientific world, Indian sculptors
and painters had actually retrograded in their
art and were less proficient in anatomical knowledge than the artists of Asoka's time. The only
alternative to this conclusion is that which I
propose, that at some period after the Bhārhut
and Sānchī sculptures Indian artists abandoned
purely naturalistic aims and perfected an ideal
of their own, which was, no doubt, latent in
Indian thought even earlier.

The Sānchī sculptures are supposed to cover a
period beginning from Asoka's reign, down to
about 140 B.C. It would require a whole volume
to do them justice, but, except as an important

link in the evolution of the Indian ideal, they do not belong to the scope of this work. They are, however, magnificently decorative, and provide a most wonderful picture of Indian life and thought, as described at the beginning of this chapter. The visits of the pilgrims to the sacred shrines, the stories told by the camp-fires, the fabled pre-existence of the Buddha in the form of bird and beast, and all the mysteries of the untrodden primeval forests, are revealed in a series of sculptures which, besides being most valuable for historical purposes, makes a most delightful, original Indian jungle-book. We can see, also, how strongly the idea of the essential unity of creation has taken hold of the Indian mind. For all nature is shown animated by a single purpose ; man and beast, gods and demi-gods, and the weird monsters of Indian mythology throng together to join in worship of the emblems of the Buddhist faith.

The Sānchī sculpures are, like those of Bhārhut, entirely naturalistic in the treatment of the human form. As Fergusson says :

" All the men and women represented are human beings, acting as men and women have acted in all times, and the success or failure of the representations may consequently be judged by the same rules as are applicable to the sculpture of any other place or country. Notwithstanding this, the mode of treatment is so original and local

THE EASTERN GATEWAY, SÁNCHĪ

PLATE XXX

A DRYAD FROM THE EASTERN GATEWAY, SĀNCHĪ

that it is difficult to assign it to any exact position in comparison with the arts of the Western world."

It would be better, perhaps, to cease judging Indian art by Western rules, and allow India the right of keeping her own artistic soul.

The person of the Buddha as a divine being receiving adoration is still unrepresented, though he appears as Prince Siddhartha and as an ascetic. There are some figures of primitive Indian deities, such as Śrī, the goddess of fortune, but they do not seem to suggest any connection with the dhyāna or yoga doctrine, or to represent an idealised type of body. The Indian artistic ideal, if it had been evolved at all, had not yet been adopted by Buddhism.

For European artists the greatest interest of the Sānchī sculptures, apart from their great decorative beauty, will probably be in their wonderfully truthful and skilful rendering of animal life. This is especially remarkable in the Eastern Gateway, one of the latest of the Sānchī sculptures, illustrated in Plate XXIX.

Yet some of the single detached figures are extremely good, and show a great advance on the art of Bhārhut, though the style is similar. Plate XXX is an illustration of a female figure, a dryad, perhaps the sylvan goddess invoked in the Vedas as Araṇyāni, singularly fine in movement and skilfully modelled, which forms a bracket

on the right-hand side of the same gateway.
The style of it shows no trace of the Hellenic
tradition, nor of the idealism of later Indian
sculpture. It is a piece of simple forceful realism
by Indian sculptors, before any attempt was made
to idealise the human form. Nevertheless it
would be difficult to find among the Gandhāran
sculptures anything to surpass it, either in technique or in artistic feeling.

Though the wooden forms of construction are
retained, the later sculptures of Sānchī, of which
these are examples, show a perfect familiarity
with the technique of stone-carving and great
freedom of execution. The best figure sculpture
found here, taken in conjunction with that of
Bhārhut, make it abundantly clear that before
the Sānchī gateways were finished, or before any
of the Gandhāran sculptures were executed,
India had developed an original school of sculpture, and was no longer dependent upon foreign
aid, as it was, to some extent, in the time of
Asoka. Indian art continued to assimilate foreign
elements, as every living art will. The Gandhāran
sculptors, no doubt, sometimes found employment in India proper, but they did not come there
as teachers, for India had nothing to learn from
them in technique, and she deliberately chose
ideals different from those of Greece.

The next important series of sculptures representing early Indian life and history are those of

Amarāvatī,[1] a Buddhist settlement on the banks
of the Krishna River, in Madras, and probably one
of the starting-points of the adventurous emi-
grants who colonised Sumatra, Java, and Cambodia. These sculptures are attributed to the
last half of the second century A.D., so there is
an interval of something like three centuries
between them and the later Sānchī sculptures.
It is obvious that a great deal of Indian sculpture
must have been produced in the interval, but
very little of it remains, no doubt for the same
reason that hardly anything has been found
before the time of Asoka, namely, because most
of it was executed in the wood of the trees consecrated to Vedic ritual.

Asoka's immediate successors did not continue
his zealous propaganda of Buddhism, so Indian
builders and sculptors naturally reverted to the
material most convenient for them. In the
meantime, however, on the north-west frontier
of India, the Indo-Baktrian school of Gandhāra
arose. Gandhāra was a country in which suitable
stone for building and sculpture was more plentiful than wood ; so while all the wooden, or semi-
wooden, buildings constructed in India in this
period have totally disappeared, the stone and
brick monasteries and the stūpas of Gandhāra

---

[1] Some of them are now in the British Museum, a few in the
Indian Museum, Calcutta, but most of the finest and best preserved
are in the Central Museum, Madras.

have left a great deal of their rich sculptures to posterity. This, and the fact that Gandhāra was closer to the outskirts of the Roman Empire, and therefore more susceptible to Græco-Roman influences than India, have given the Gandhāran school a rather fictitious importance in the history of Indian art. To understand this early period of Indian art rightly we must always bear in mind that for every monument in stone which now exists, there were perhaps a thousand in less permanent materials, which have completely disappeared.

The Amarāvatī sculptures show the Buddha for the first time in Indian art as a divine being receiving worship, and as the type of Buddha image closely resembles that of Gandhāra, Professor Grünwedel and other archæologists infer that the Græco-Roman artists of the Kushān Empire supplied Indian Buddhists with the ideal of their divinity. But the Amarāvatī Buddha is not the Indian ideal of divinity : it is a transitional type. In all the art of Amarāvatī we see Indian sculpture passing from the naturalistic school of the Asokan epoch into the idealistic school in which Indian art reached its highest expression. The simple, unsophisticated naturalism of the Bhārhut and Sānchī sculptures is here beginning to change into a very pronounced style of an academic character, but wholly different from the style of Gandhāra, though in

PLATE XXXI

RELIEF FROM AMARĀVATĪ

(From the base of the Great Stūpa)

the detail Gandhāran or Græco-Roman types frequently occur.

One of the finest and best preserved of the Amarāvatī reliefs is a sculptured slab from the base of the stūpa (Plate XXXI) now in the Madras Museum. It represents the stūpa itself, surrounded with its rail, and with a crowd of adoring spirits, the *vidhyādharas*, hovering round its summit. These figures are perhaps the most beautifully designed of all, and they show clearly the idealistic treatment which had developed in Indian sculpture since the Asokan period. The flying movement of these heavenly spirits is conceived with rare artistic feeling and a thorough grasp of the mechanism of the human body, although the details of the muscular system are purposely suppressed.

In the Tusita heavens above the stūpa, supported by the two mystic world-pillars on either side, the Buddha sits enthroned receiving worship. Here and elsewhere in the reliefs he is clad in the same loose robe as the Gandhāran Buddhas. This partially conceals the form and makes the idealistic treatment less conspicuous than it is in the almost nude figures of the *vidhyādharas*, or in the Buddha of later Indian sculpture illustrated previously. In the small upright panels on the right and left of the throne are two very expressive figures of a Nāga Rājā and his wife worshipping. They are well drawn and modelled with more anatomical precision than the *vidhyā-dharas*, as if to suggest a contrast between ordinary mortal form and the divine one.

This distinction, whether it is intentional or not in this particular case, is not observed throughout the reliefs ; nor is it characteristic of Indian art as a whole. But it is easy to understand that the recognition of a special type of beauty for divine beings would very speedily resolve itself into a general idealisation of the human form in the same direction ; the first step being its application as a mark of distinction for persons of high rank, and the next its adoption as a general academic formula.

The Amarāvatī reliefs, so far from being inspired by Western ideals, indicate the definite evolution of distinctly Indian ones : except for a few obviously borrowed details and motifs there is very little that is foreign about them. The style and whole mode of artistic expression are developments of the Bhārhut and Sānchī school, as can be seen in the beautiful group from the British Museum, Plate XXXII. The slim-waisted figure standing by the horse, probably intended for Prince Siddhartha, shows the tendency towards Indian idealism. The two female figures, charmingly natural in pose, are ordinary human beings like those of Bhārhut and Sānchī, but the execution shows no trace of the Western academic style. The exaggerated thinness of

RELIEF FROM AMARĀVATĪ

102]

the legs of all the figures was, perhaps, less marked when the sculptures had their finishing coat of fine plaster, though thin legs, like an antelope's, were marks of beauty both for men and women in Indian art.

The foreign elements in all of the Amarāvatī sculptures are not more conspicuous than those usually found in the art of any country which from its imperial position has become a centre of attraction for people of many and diverse nationalities. Nowhere do they justify the assumption that Indian art at this period was in Græco-Roman leading-strings. There is this in common with the Gandhāran sculptures and those of Amarāvatī—that both were inspired by the monastic schools of northern India ; the former employing foreign agents, the latter mostly Indian. The foreign artists of Gandhāra were naturally slower in absorbing Indian impressions, derived from the philosophical schools, than the native artists. The great culture-centres of Asia were at this time the Indian universities of Takshasila, Benares, Sridhanya Kataka, on the banks of the Krishna, and Nālanda : their influence was supreme, and compared with it the whole influence of Hellenism in Indian art may be taken as a negligible factor. It is to the direct teaching and influence of these great educational centres, rather than to the occasional intrusion of foreign suggestions and foreign technique, that we must look for an explanation of the development of Indian artistic ideals. For certainly the teaching of the Mahāyāna doctrine by Nāgārjuna, and the infusion of Brahmanical ideas into Buddhism, were the influences which shaped the ideals of Indian art, not the migration of Western artistic ideas eastwards. India was not then in a state of pupilage, but the teacher of all Asia, and she only borrowed Western ideas to mould them to her own way of thinking. " What Cluny and Clairvaux were to France in the Middle Ages," says Fergusson, " Nālanda was to Central India—the depository of all true learning and the foundation from which it spread to all other lands of the faithful." The whole range of education in these great universities was schemed and co-ordinated with a breadth and largeness undreamt of in modern India. There were schools of painting, sculpture, and handicrafts as well as of mathematics, astronomy, medicine, and other sciences ; at Nālanda religion and philosophy were taught from a hundred chairs. Not less greatly planned were the equipment and environment of the colleges. Hiuen Tsang, who resided at Nālanda for several years, describes it as " an enchanting abode." It had been in existence for seven centuries when he visited it. Six successive Indian kings had devoted their pious efforts to building and adorning it. The last one reorganised the work of his predecessors, opened a number of halls for conferences, and surrounded the whole convent with a single wall. One gate opened into the great college which the Chinese pilgrim thus describes :

" The richly adorned towers were arranged in regular order ; the pavilions, decorated with coral, appeared like painted hill-tops ; the soaring domes reached up to the clouds, and the pinnacles of the temples seemed to be lost in the mist of the morning. From their windows one could watch the movements of the winds and clouds, and above their lofty roofs the sun and moon could be seen in conjunction.

" All around pools of translucent water shone with the open petals of the blue lotus-flower ; here and there the lovely kanaka-trees hung down their deep red blossoms ; and groves of dark mango-trees spread their shade between them. In the different courts the houses of the monks were each four stories in height. The pavilions had pillars ornamented with dragons, and beams resplendent with all the colours of the rainbow—rafters richly carved—columns ornamented with jade, painted red and richly chiselled, and balustrades of carved open work. The lintels of the doors were decorated with elegance and the roof covered with glazed tiles of brilliant colours, which multiplied themselves by reflection, and varied the effect at every moment in a thousand ways." [1]

[1] " La Vie de Hiouen Thsang," by Stanislas Julien, pp. 150, 151.

9

The groves of mango-trees and the immense tanks still remain as memorials of this splendid convent. There were thousands of these convents in India, though this was the finest of them all. To them students flocked from all parts of Asia, and from them went out the missionaries who brought Indian philosophy, science, and art to the most distant parts of the continent, China, Korea, and Japan.

Among such surroundings and by such influences were nurtured and developed the culture and ideals which created the great monuments of Indian art, and such was the respect for the dignity of learning inspired by them that, according to the Chinese pilgrim, no single instance of deliberate rebellion against the rules had been known at Nālanda during the seven hundred years since the foundation of the college. Apparently they possessed a secret of which modern India is ignorant. But could love of the *alma mater* ever grow up among the squalid, hideous surroundings, unkept and uncared for, of most Indian colleges?

The Amarāvatī reliefs are considered by Fergusson and Professor Grünwedel to represent the culminating point in Indian sculpture. But this view can only be held by those who regard as decadence, instead of a new development on a higher plane of thought, the departure from European canons which here took place. Indian

sculptors reached much higher imaginative flights
and achieved greater technical triumphs, but,
after Amarāvatī, they adopted an ideal of beauty
totally different from that of Greece. They
never attempted such a minute scientific investi-
gation of the human structure as the sculptors
of the Italian Renaissance made, because it
would have been useless to them in perfecting an
idealistic creation based upon imaginative and
artistic feeling, rather than upon scientific facts.

Though they are far from showing the highest
flights of Indian sculptors, there is much beautiful
work in them. The traditions of Sānchī were
upheld in the most delightful studies of animal
life, combined with extremely refined conventional ornament. The most varied movements
of the human figure are drawn and modelled
with great freedom and skill. The action and
grouping of the figures are singularly animated
and expressive. In skilful composition, especially
in the design of crowds, a point in which Indian
artists always excelled, they far surpass the
contemporary school of Gandhāra, and although
the sentiment seems sometimes rather forced and
artificial, it is much more genuine than the conventional, smug pietism of the Græco-Roman, or
Indo-Roman, sculptures.

In Indian art they take much the same place
as Cellini's work holds in the sculpture of the
Italian Renaissance. But technically the two

rails must be considered as painted *rilievos*, rather than true sculpture. The artists relied upon colour, instead of alternation of light and shade, to give emphasis and variety to the composition. Now that the colour has entirely disappeared, the effect of the sculpture viewed at a distance is comparatively cold and lifeless, in spite of the prodigious amount of labour bestowed upon it.

The Indian ideal which we see in process of evolution at Amarāvatī was finally perfected several centuries later. The various types of it have been discussed in the previous chapters. The next great series of sculptured reliefs in which Indian real life is vividly portrayed are those which adorned the great Buddhist shrine of Borobudur, Java's Kailāsa temple. These must be dealt with in greater detail in the next chapter.

CHAPTER VIII

BOROBUDUR—THE KAILĀSA OF JAVA

THE native chronicles of Java, says Sir Stamford Raffles in his History, date the earliest arrival of colonists from India about A.D. 75, when a prince of Gujarāt led an expedition to the island, which did not, however, succeed in making a permanent settlement. In 603, they narrate, a great fleet convoying some 5,000 men, including agriculturists and artificers, established a Gujarātī dynasty in the centre of the island, under whose rule most of the great monuments, including the city of Prambānam and the famous stūpa of Borobudur, were built. But modern archæological research has revealed the fact that about 750, the approximate date of the building of Borobudur, the then ruling power in Central Java had been expelled by a rival Indian dynasty, the Cailendras, established in Sumatra; the Cailendras, therefore, must be regarded as the builders of Borobudur.

The famous stūpa, the greatest Buddhist monument of the world, has a character of its own quite

distinct from any known Indian prototypes.
It may rightly be called Indo-Javanese in style,
for it was characteristic of the ancient Vedic
culture, which spread over so large a part of Asia,
that it always adapted itself to its local environment. Yet both in its structural design and in
its splendid sculptured decoration, this great monument of Mahāyāna Buddhism in Java is inspired
by Indian thought and Indian craftsmanship.

The original Indian stūpa of Vedic times was
the funeral mound raised over the ashes of an
Aryan chieftain. The early Buddhist stūpas have
only the significance of a reliquary or memorial,
enclosed by a railing to prevent the intrusion of
evil spirits, the umbrella which crowned the
summit being only the emblem of the Buddha's
rank as a Sākyan prince. But gradually the
stūpa was transformed into a religious or metaphysical symbol. The hemispherical dome
became the symbol of the inverted sky-lotus.
Its pinnacle, a series of umbrellas, piled one over
the other and carved underneath with lotuses,
stood for the higher spheres, culminating in the
planes unconditioned by form and free from
sensual desire. When the Buddha himself was
deified and translated to Mt. Kailāsa, the central
point of the world Yantra, the stūpa was con-
verted into a shrine for his image, and Siva's
Himalayan hermitage became the final goal for the
Buddhist as well as for the Hindu pilgrim. The

Brahmanical doctrine of Yoga, at first regarded by Buddhist teachers as rank heresy, was adopted by Mahāyāna philosophy and inspired the idealism of the Buddhist artist and craftsman. Just as the artist sought by the practice of Yoga to visualise the image of the deity, so the builder, in designing the shrine where the image was to be placed, kept ever in his mind's eye the holy shrine where the Divine Yogi himself dwelt. The traditional rite of circumambulation of the temple, as well as the pilgrim's journey to Kailāsa, became a symbolic act of Yoga, the following of the spiral ascent which brought the Yogi to Nirvāna.

When the pilgrim had climbed the hill on which Borobudur is built, and the long flights of steps leading to the mysterious hidden shrine which crowns the summit, the prospect would bring many reminiscences of the great northern pilgrimage of India. A wide, fertile plain stretches beneath, like the Ganges Valley at the foot of the Himalayas. In the distance majestic mountain tops tower into the sky ; not, indeed, the shining snow-peaks, sources of holy rivers, outwardly so infinitely calm, but covering the intense creative energy latent even in Nature's most peaceful moods. Here are seen grim, grey volcanoes, both extinct and active, which ever seem to threaten with destruction the fair edifice of the Creator. But to the Indian thinker the contrast would seem only to illustrate Nature's law, symbolised in the cosmic Yantra with its two similar equilateral triangles, which interlaced keep the universe in equipoise.[1] Siva was here also, as He was at Kailāsa, only in His destructive mood.

Convincing proof that such recollections occurred to the Indian colonists of Java is given by the fact that the highest mountain-top is named Smeru, after Sumeru, the mythical mountain of the Himalayas, while other volcanoes, like Himalayan peaks, bear the names of the Pāndava pilgrims. The principal river of Central Java is named after the Himalayan river Sarayu, upon the banks of which Rāma's famous city stood.[2]

The builders of Borobudur, therefore, when they created a splendid shrine for all the Buddhas of the Mahāyāna pantheon, followed the Indian tradition and designed it after the cosmic Yantra, used in the ritual of Yoga, but in three dimensions instead of two. The plane Yantra, Fig. 2, when constructed in three dimensions, becomes a hemispheroid, like an early Indian stūpa, with the generating point, the Bindu, or Kailāsa, at the top (Fig. 3). It is used in this form in modern Hindu ritual, and is the symbol of the Brah-

[1] The equilateral triangle, standing on its apex, is a symbol of water; reversed it becomes a symbol of fire.

[2] Dr. J. P. Vogel, " Influences of Indian Art " (Indian Society Publication), p. 37.

māṇḍa, the cosmic egg or spheroid, with its seven upper and seven lower planes ; but only the upper half is worshipped, as representing the earthly and heavenly spheres.

In the stūpa of Borobudur this cosmic symbol is constructed on a colossal scale. It was designed with a square base, like the miniature Yantra used in ancient and modern ritual, and arranged in seven planes after the metaphysical concept. Constructional necessities compelled the builders to flatten the curve of the spheroid considerably, so that pilgrims in their circumambulation might be able to reach the summit. Those who followed the whole procession path up to the stūpa's crowning pinnacle were performing symbolically the same rite as the Buddhist pilgrim of to-day, when he first visits the sacred places associated with the various lives of the Blessed One on earth, and then climbs the heights of Kailāsa to bow down in worship, as if in the presence of the Lord Buddha.

In exactly the same way the pilgrims at Borobudur, when they entered the lowest procession path, began to pass in review the previous lives of the Buddha, as told in the jātakas, and the story of his last rebirth. Then, as they mounted to the higher circular terraces, they entered the regions of formlessness, the transcendental Himalayas, where the images of the Dhyāni-Buddhas (Plate I) were only dimly visible through

the lattice-work of their bell-shaped Yantras
(Fig. 1). Finally, at the summit, they reached
Kailāsa, the centre of the cosmic Yantra, where
Gautama Buddha sat calling earth to witness his
Enlightenment, as he had done under the bodhi-
tree at Gāyā, but invisible, like Siva in his Himalayan cell, except to the adept in Yoga ; for
the image was entirely embedded in the masonry
of the cupola which crowns the stūpa, so that no

FIG. 4.—Skyline of Borobudur.

human eyes could see it, nor human hands touch
it.   It was thus that the creators of Borobudur
symbolised the highest insight, the supreme goal
of the devout Buddhist.

The skyline of Borobudur (Fig. 4), with its
myriad pinnacles, like mountain peaks, suggested
the worlds innumerable from which all the Buddhas
had flocked on that great day when Gautama
proclaimed his Buddhahood.   But architecturally
Borobudur, in its incomplete and ruined state, is
far less impressive than Ankhor Vat in Cambodia ;

chiefly on account of its stunted proportions, which
are partly due to the exigencies of the procession
paths, and partly to a miscalculation in engineer-
ing which obliged the builders to prevent the
collapse of the whole edifice by strengthening it
with a solid band of masonry at the base.   The
height of the walls of the lowest terrace in the
original project was thus considerably reduced.
Nevertheless, as the master builder imagined it,
with its vast glittering white walls, painted
reliefs, and gilded pinnacles and cupolas, it was
a noble conception worthy of one of the world's
great spiritual Teachers ; a poet's dream of India's
heavenly city, Himalaya, the Abode of Snow.

A detailed description of this great architectural
tour de force does not come within the scope of
this book.   The chief glory of Borobudur now is
its wonderful series of sculptures, extending in
the aggregate for a length of nearly three miles,
and expounding in ordered sequence the mythology and philosophy of Mahāyāna Buddhism.
For the devout Buddhist who paced these
sculptured galleries they were illustrated scrip-
tures, which even the most ignorant could read,
telling in living words the life-story and message
of the Master.   We have discussed already the
Indian idealised type of Divinity which is represented on the monument in countless images of
Buddhas and Bodhisattvas in high and low
relief, sculptured in panels and placed in niches

above the different galleries. We are now only concerned with the reliefs along the procession paths which exhibit the Indian sculptor's highest achievements in the treatment of scenes of real, or quasi-real, life. Fortunately, though some have suffered from exposure to the weather, they have escaped the ruthless vandalism to which nearly all works of art in India have been subject.

These reliefs give, in the upper half, one hundred and twenty scenes from the life of the Buddha, following the text of the Lalitavistara, and, in the lower half, a similar number from the jātakas —the legends of his previous existences. Tradition gives only the name of the chief master-builder, one Guṇadharma.[1] The Indian master-builder is always a skilled carver. Doubtless some of the principal sculptures were from his own chisel, but in such a vast undertaking a great number of apprentices and inferior crafts-men must have been employed, over whose work the chief designers could only exercise general supervision. In fact the sculptures show a much more uneven quality of technique than is found in small-scale monuments like Amarāvatī, but the extraordinary beauty of the best of them can be seen in the reproductions given in Plates XXXIII to XXXVIII. They are from a splendid

[1] Dr. N. J. Krom, " The Life of the Buddha on the Stūpa of Barabudur."

set of photographs made in 1872 for the Batavian Society of Arts and Sciences by Mr. J. van Kinsbergen.

Evidently there is a close kinship between them and the sculptures of Amarāvatī, but the Borobudur craftsmen have been inspired by the colossal scale of the building to adopt a much more spacious and dignified style of design. To compare them with the Panathenaic frieze of the Parthenon would serve no useful purpose, though as artistic achievements of the highest class the best Borobudur sculptures would not suffer by the comparison. There is as little kinship between the academic refinements of the Parthenon sculptures and this supremely devout and spontaneous art as there is between Indian and Hellenic religious thought. They are much more closely allied in feeling and expression to the sculptures of Donatello and those of the best Italian masters of the fourteenth and fifteenth centuries.

A very near parallel may be found in the celebrated bronze doors of the Baptistery of Florence, by Lorenzo Ghiberti, one of the great masterpieces of Italian art, of which Michelangelo is reported to have said that they were " fit to be the gates of Paradise." In these gates a number of Biblical scenes are treated in a series of relief panels with accessories similar to those used by the Borobudur sculptors, i.e. the figures are accompanied by representations of temples, houses, trees, clouds, water, and landscape.

The Italian master achieved a technical triumph which won for him the rapturous applause of the *virtuosi* of his day, yet by the use of perspective and of an excessive number of planes of relief, in the attempt to produce the illusion of pictorial effects, he sacrificed breadth and dignity and overstepped the limitations of plastic art. In spite of its extraordinary technical qualities the main impression given by Ghiberti's masterpiece is that the artist was more concerned in exhibiting his skill to his fellow-citizens than in producing the most perfect and reverent rendering of the sacred subjects.

The Borobudur sculptors, with much deeper reverence and less self-consciousness, show conclusively that art is greater than artifice. The very simplicity and unaffected naiveté of their style are much more impressive and convincing than the elaborate efforts of the Italian master, who, with all his wonderful technique, is far behind in imagination and poetic feeling. Especially in the magnificent conventionalism of the accessories—the trees, buildings, ships, etc.— does the art of Borobudur rise above the art of Ghiberti. Western artists, also, before their intuitive faculties were atrophied by the pedantic teaching of the schools, saw that their conventional perspective, not strictly bound by optical laws, gave a much greater richness and variety in design. That is why the pre-Renaissance art of Europe has generally a much finer decorative quality than the art of the Renaissance, or the academic art of modern Europe.

The great charm of the Borobudur sculptures lies in their absolute truth of expression, a truthfulness which is the more conspicuous because the artists have not tied themselves to the petty rules and regulations upon which the modern dilettante critic so often bases his judgement of works of art. What modern academician would dare to disregard the relative proportion between human figures and the accessory trees, houses, temples, elephants, oxen, and carts as these men have done—not because they did not *know*, but because they felt the story must be told in that way ? And yet the disproportion does not jar, it only contributes marvellously to the strength of the story-telling and to the richness of the decorative effect.

The artists who conceived these sculptures were not aiming at the applause of their fellow-men, but trying to tell the story of the Master in the way they conceived He had told it, offering their labour and skill as a devout gift to His shrine. Art seems to reach its highest and go deepest when all that is small and common is excluded, when the effort of the artist is invisible, and when nature, purified by the God-given powers of man, is, as it were, re-born. The simple life these men led left them in peace to concentrate their whole soul on their work, and kept their minds free and able to listen to the voices of nature and of their own inspiration—the soul of nature speaking to the soul of men.

They loved and reverenced the Buddha with all their heart, and through the directness and strength of this feeling, and because there was nothing to jar on it in their life and surroundings, they, with the great gifts they had, could show what they felt without feebleness and without faltering. The spiritual power of their art has broken the chains of technical rules, risen above all thought of what critics call right or wrong, and speaks with divinely inspired words straight to the heart of the listener. In this heaven-born quality of inspiration European art has rarely equalled, and never excelled, the art of Borobudur.

Just as we have seen in the Indian ideal type, the smaller anatomical details of the figures are suppressed, but the real spark of life, the essence of feeling, is wonderfully manifested. Every group and every figure are absolutely true and sincere in expression of face, gesture, and pose of body ; and the actions which link the various groups and single figures together are strongly and simply told, without any effort or striving for effect—it was so, because so it could only be.

RELIEF AT BOROBUDUR

The lower panel in Plate XXXIII is one of the most beautiful and perfectly preserved of the whole series. We think at once of Tanagra. Yes, but the pretty domestic art of Tanagra produced nothing so great as this. It is Tanagra art, without its coquetry, chastened and strengthened by a profound religious sentiment. The scene is one which may be witnessed every day in any Indian village, but the inspiration of the art which created such a masterpiece lives no longer.

It is only a group of Indian women drawing water from the village tank, under the shade of the sacred tree next to the village temple. One of them bending over the lotus-covered water is just filling her vessel, watching it intently as she draws it up with her left hand, while her right is raised to grasp it when it comes within reach. Some with their vessels filled and balanced truly on their heads are already moving off with queenly steps, and wend their way towards the village shrine. Others are approaching the water with their empty vessels. And one apart from the rest is kneeling at the foot of the Bodhisattva and receiving instructions from him.

The story comes from the jātakas. It tells how the Buddha was once born as the Prince Sudhana, son of a king of northern India. Sudhana falls in love with a fairy princess, who, having incautiously flown down to earth from the

10

Himalayas, had been captured by a hunter with his magic lasso. The prince took her to his father's court, but a crafty Brahman minister having plotted to take her life, the queen helps her to escape. She flies away home, but leaves with a hermit in the forest a ring and instructions by which the prince might find his way into the Himalayan fairyland. After a long and difficult journey the prince reaches it and meets the princess's handmaidens going to fetch water for her bath.

In the series of thirty panels which tell the story is this most delightful one, where the prince sitting under a tree talks to one of the girls and drops the ring into her pitcher, so that the princess might know of his arrival. The artist with a rare touch of genius has conveyed, in the gracious figure of Sudhana and the reverent attitude of the hand-maiden, a subtle suggestion of the higher life towards which the Prince was aiming. We know now that in another life he will become the En-lightened One and the Teacher of the Law.

How marvellously the whole scene lives and moves, and what an atmosphere of purity, freshness, and womanly grace breathes through it all. We seem to feel the brightness of the Indian morning and hear the twittering of the birds as they fly from tree to tree and hover round the temple roof. Every figure is full of unconscious grace and dignity ; every movement

RELIEF AT BOROBUDUR

helps, but there is no posing for effect, no effort
of the artist to show his cleverness. The simplicity of the treatment is as wonderful as its
strength.   Where Ghiberti or any modern European sculptor would use half-a-dozen planes of
relief, the Indian artist is content with one or two,
and tells his story with much greater vividness
and truthful feeling.

And over all there is an undefinable sense of
reverent adoration, for the beauty of nature and
for the divine wisdom which created it.   This is
the leading motif in the music of all these panels.
It is repeated again and again in different keys
and different chords, every note and every phrase
helping to make one harmonious sequence of
praise and thankfulness.

The upper panel in the same plate is one of the
series which tells the marvellous story of the
Buddha's last appearance on earth. Queen
Māyā, seated in her palace, on the right, has sent a
messenger to ask the king to come to her at once,
to explain the wonderful dream she has dreamt.
King Shuddhodana, to whom a heavenly voice
has already whispered the news, receives the
messenger as he stands under the state umbrella,
with his ministers in attendance, pondering over
the strange event.   The royal elephant, a noble
beast, salutes his master, and seems to say,
" Come, let us go to the palace ! "

In the upper panel of Plate XXXIV the King

is distributing rewards to ten Brahmans who interpreted the dream. There is wonderful descriptive power and truth of expression in the lower panel of the same plate, a continuation of the story of Prince Sudhana, showing the nautch party performing at his wedding festivities. The dominant note in the composition is given by the Devadāsi, dancing Siva's dance in front of the canopy under which the bridegroom and his bride are seated. The close grouping of the musicians on the left, all absorbed in the accompaniment of the dance, balanced by the group of animals and attendants, all intently listening on the right, helps to fix attention on the superb figure of the dancer whose rhythmic movements and gestures interpret the cosmic law. The Prince himself also listens to the music, but in a pensive mood, for his thoughts are far, far away. This again is a perfectly true note. The instinct which led the artist to express this touches the centre of true feeling.

The two panels in the next illustration, Plate XXXV, show the same superlative sense of beauty and power of grouping figures together to express varying feelings and emotions. The upper one represents Queen Māyā, seated in her state car and hastening with her retinue to the Lumbini Gardens, where, as she had been told in a dream, her son, who was to be the salvation of the world, should be born. The male attend-

RELIEF AT BOROBUDUR

124]

ants surround the car in zealous care of their
royal mistress, clearing the path in front of any
untoward or unseemly thing, and holding the
insignia of royalty proudly over her, while the
ladies in her train follow behind in lively converse
on the coming event.   The expression of queenly
dignity in Māyā and the eager expectancy in the
throng of her attendants, as well as the movement
of the whole procession, are perfectly given.
The lower panel, belonging to the jātaka series,
shows a princess inside a temple, making offerings
at the shrine.   Her attendant ladies, waiting
outside, make an exquisite group, designed with
consummate art.   It is one of the gems of Borobudur, evidently the work of a master-craftsman.

We now pass by over twenty panels, all well
designed as decoration, but lacking the distinctive touch of the master.   We must remember
that a great monument like this was a school of
traditional craftsmanship, in which the sons and
pupils of the masters of the age were allotted their
share of the work under their guru's eye, and
thus learnt their craft.

In none of these scenes is there any set form or
mannerism in the grouping, such as we often
observe in Ghiberti's art and in the composition
of many of the best Italian masters.   The spacing
of the figures and their accessories in the panel
is by no means haphazard : it is all admirably
designed.   But these Borobudur sculptors have

known how to convey the essence of truth, as it is found in nature, without obtruding their own personality or the technique of their craft. Their art, used only in the service of truth and religion, has made their hands the obedient tools of a heaven-sent inspiration ; and their unique power of realising thus, with a depth and sincerity unsurpassed in the art of any land, gives them a right to rank among the greatest of the symbolists in the whole history of art.

Again we must pass by a number of sculptured panels of no special artistic interest : the master-craftsman's touch is wanting, though the uncritical eyes of the pilgrims would not notice the difference, for the story is intelligible and never lacks interest for them. This is not a record of the dead past, but the realisation of the great Teacher's living presence. Then we come to another fine group, the upper panel in Plate XXXVI, showing Prince Siddhartha in the archery tournament, competing with other Sākya lords, his cousins, for the hand of the fair Yasodharā. The scene is described by Sir Edwin Arnold in " The Light of Asia " :

> Then Nanda challenged for the arrow-test
> And set a brazen drum six gows away,
> Ardjuna six and Devadatta eight ;
> But Prince Siddhartha bade them set his drum
> Ten gows from off the line, until it seemed
> A cowry-shell for target. Then they loosed

RELIEF AT BOROBUDUR

And Nanda pierced his drum, Ardjuna his,
And Devadatta drove a well-aimed shaft
Through both sides of his mark, so that the crowd
Marvelled and cried ; sweet Yasodharā
Dropped the gold sari o'er her fearful eyes,
Lest she should see the Prince's arrow fail.

The bow first offered him Siddhartha broke in testing, and then called for one " more fit for Sākya lords to use "—the famous bow of Siva, kept in the temple, which no man had yet been able to draw :

Twice Siddhartha tried
Its strength across his knee, then spake—" Shoot now
With this, my cousins ! " but they could not bring
The stubborn arms a hair's breadth nearer use ;
Then the Prince, lightly leaning, bent the bow.

.   .   .   .   .   .

Then lifting fair a shaft, he drew and loosed,
And the keen arrow clave the sky and drave
Right through that farthest drum, nor stayed its flight
But skimmed the plain beyond, past reach of eye.

The artist has not made an exhibition of his own skill : he knew how to conceal his art. Nor has he tried to indicate any supernatural quality in the Prince's strength. He just shows us the incident as it might have occurred in the court life of his time. The simplicity and unconventionality with which the tale is told gives it its charm, and the student of the present day who reads these panels can enjoy the artist's power, just as the myriads of devout pilgrims who reverently paced the procession paths of Borobudur did in bygone days.

Again we must pass by a long stretch of richly sculptured wall, with only a panel here and there which calls for special remark. Then we find another gem, Plate XXXVII, in the upper part of which the Prince having at last attained Nirvāna, bathes in the River Nairañjanā. Here we have no longer the man with human desires and aims, but the Buddha in the full glory of his divinity. All his struggles and trials are finished now : he has passed through all the gates of difficulty and doubting. Now he is the noble, purified soul, in a noble body filled with heavenly bliss.

Every creature that comes near him is conscious of it. The spirits of the upper air, the Vidhyādharas and Siddhas, whose voices the pilgrims heard so often in their wanderings, flock round him showering scented flowers on the river, feeling and rejoicing in the power of purity which goes out of him. The Nāgas, the water-sprites, raise their heads to do him homage. On the other side of the river, three of the Devas, in the attire of Javanese princes, prostrate themselves before him, and reverently scoop up water, like pilgrims, to carry away with them to their divine mansions.

The doe from the forest knows at once that her Lord and Protector has come, He who in His boundless love once offered His life for hers. She

RELIEF AT BOROBUDUR

RELIEF AT BOROBUDUR

whispers the joyful tidings to her little one, which turns its head in curiosity to look upon Him whom all nature worships. The lower half of the panel, with its magnificently designed ship in a storm, tells another jātaka story, typical of the adventurous life of the Indian colonists. The sailors are trying desperately to furl sails and bring the ship to anchor. On land a benevolent householder and his wife, under the grateful shade of the palm-grove surrounding the house, appear to be distributing food to the survivors of the wreck. The contrast between the fury of the ocean and the peaceful serenity of the land is drawn with the faithfulness and sincerity of feeling characteristic of all these reliefs. The two different incidents and different moods are ingeniously knit together in one rich and harmonious decorative scheme.

The last of the illustrations selected to show the work of the master-sculptor at Borobudur, Plate XXXVIII, is one of a series representing scenes in the Tusita heavens, where, according to Mahāyāna teaching, all Bodhisattvas are born before they appear in the world, and where Maitreya, the coming Buddha, now lives.

Here, also, the Buddha, Gautama, having finished his incarnations on earth and accomplished his Pari-nirvāna, is said to have gone to teach and convert his mother Māyā, who died a week after his birth. This is probably the scene

represented in the panel. The Buddha, enthroned in all the glory of his divinity under a
splendid canopy, is preaching the Law to Māyā,
who sits in happy ecstasy listening to the inspired
words of her son.

The two symbolic trees, magnificently conven-
tionalised, the doves and sacred birds which
hover overhead, contribute greatly to the richness
of the decorative scheme ; but the rare genius
of the artist is most conspicuous in the charming
group of the Queen's five attendants, leaning
forward as far as respect for their royal mistress
will permit, and straining their ears so that no
word of the Divine Truth may escape them.

Were it not that the reputation of works of
art in Europe depends far more upon the label
attached to them by the pedantic tradition of
our so-called classical education than upon their
intrinsic merits, these wonderful sculptures would
not have remained in obscurity so long. Mr. van
Kinsbergen's photographs, taken in 1872, were
buried in the libraries of six learned societies for
thirty-six years, before artists in Europe took
notice of them. But it can hardly be doubted that
had these sculptures been labelled " Greek,"
" Roman," or " Italian, " the volumes of criticism
and commentaries on them would have filled many
libraries ; casts of them would be found in every
European art-school and museum ; tourists would
have flocked to inscribe their names on them or

chip off fragments as souvenirs ; art-dealers and American millionaires would have jostled one another in eagerness to possess them.   But being only Indo-Javanese and memorials of a great Asiatic culture, they were for long years totally unappreciated, though well-known to oriental savants.

And while the living traditions of this great art still survive in India, we establish schools to teach Indians sculpture and painting as they are taught in Europe, and send out sculptors and painters to decorate Indian buildings, under the pretext that we are helping to elevate the taste of the Indian public.

Europe of the present day has far more to learn from India in art than to teach.   Religious art in Europe is altogether lost : it perished in our so-called Renaissance.   In India the true spirit of it still lives.

Quite apart from its purely æsthetic quality there is in an art like this an ethical value which modern India for the most part seems unable to understand and utilise.   It is just in this ethical principle that modern education on classical lines misconstrues the spirit of classical culture and art.   Every national art is an expression of national character, and when we compare the devout and reverent outlook upon Nature shown in these Borobudur sculptures with the utter vulgarity of modern India, as we have made it, it is only too evident that in one respect our education falls immeasurably behind that of Greece and of ancient India, through the neglect of Plato's injunction " to use the beauties of earth as steps along which we mount upwards."

India, vulgarised by modern education and by the sordid ideals of modern commercialism, will never compensate humanity for the passing of India with its love of beauty—the perfect law of Nature, in which science and art are one.

CHAPTER IX

HINDU ART IN JAVA AND CAMBODIA.
PORTRAITURE

THE Borobudur sculptures are in some respects unique, both in the perfection of their art and in the good fortune which has preserved them from wanton destruction. The obscurity into which the great monument fell was its best protection, saving it from the fate of so many other masterpieces of Indian art. No fanatics, either European or native, have laid sacrilegious hands upon it ; no enterprising builders have made use of it as a stone quarry, or as materials for lime ; no railway contractors or energetic public works officers have broken up its splendid sculptures for ballast or road-mending. What it has suffered has been from natural causes, the destructive influences of a tropical climate, from earthquake, or from mere neglect. In recent years, under the zealous care of the Netherlands India Archæological Department, it has been judiciously restored and is now safe from any vandalism.

Just as in India proper, Buddhist and Brahmanical art in Java had a common philosophy and a common technical tradition. The cult of Siva, says Dr. Vogel,[1] flourished in Java side by side with Buddhism, and, as we have seen in the design of Borobudur, the ideas of both religious schools intermingled.

Some of the finest Brahmanical images of Java have been illustrated in Plates XIV, XX, and XXVI. They often bear a distinct impress of Indian origin, and may have been sometimes direct importations from the most famous Indian centres of temple craft, or sometimes the work of royal craftsmen brought from India to give distinction to the great building enterprises of the Indo-Javanese dynasties. Royal courts always vied with each other in the skill of their artists and craftsmen : the latter were always regarded as valuable loot in war, and the loan or gift of a master-craftsman would be a most acceptable proof of friendliness in diplomatic intercourse between the rival dynasties which from time to time held command of the chief Asian sea-routes. In this way there would have been a constant flow of artistic culture from India to her great Eastern colonies, diminishing in force as the colonial rulers obtained a sufficient supply of local craftsmen to meet their artistic requirements. But both in Java and Cambodia art gradually

[1] " Influences of Indian Art," p. 68.

RĀMĀYANA RELIEF, PRAMBĀNAM, JAVA

sank down again to its original primitive level when Indian thought ceased to control and inspire it.

Prambānam, the ancient capital of Central Java, has a triple-shrined Saiva temple, dedicated to the Trimūrti, differing in structure from the Borobudur stūpa, but surrounded, like the latter, by an enclosed procession path, on the walls of which is exhibited a long series of sculptured reliefs for the edification of worshippers. The subject, in this case, is taken from the Hindu epic, the Rāmāyana, which was current folk-lore in Java as it was throughout India.

These sculptures are probably two or three centuries later in date than the great Buddhist monument. They mark the climax and the beginning of the decline of Indo-Javanese art. Though there are passages of magnificent design, carried out with a wonderful richness of plastic effect, generally speaking they lack the fine simplicity and restraint of the best Borobudur sculptures. The master-craftsman's personal touch is most conspicuous in the beginning of the series, illustrated in Plates XXXIX and XL, a splendid rendering of the opening scene of the Rāma legend, of which various versions are known in India and Java. In this case we may accept Dr. Vogel's opinion that it represents the version adopted in Kālidāsa's " Raghuvamśa," in which the gods, headed by Brahmā, appeal to Vishnu to incarnate himself as Rāma, in order that the world may be saved from the wicked demon-king, Rāvana.

Vishnu is discovered in the depths of the cosmic ocean, which teems with varied forms of marine life, reclining in the formal pose of " regal ease " on the serpent Ananta, the symbol of eternity. The deity's *vahan* or vehicle, the sun-bird, Garuda, sits in his mountain-grot on the left, holding Vishnu's flower, the blue lotus. On the right of the panel the gods approach the Lord of Life with their request.

The next scene, Plate XL, brilliantly composed and evidently by the same master-mason, brings us to the court of Ayodhyā, where Rāma and his three brothers were born to King Dasaratha and his three wives. Here Dasaratha is receiving a chela of the great sage Vishvamitra, who by his Yogic power has learnt the intentions of the gods and sends him with the message that he has wonderful news for the king. The whole series of sculptures is admirably illustrated and described by Dr. Wilhelm Stutterheim in his " Rāma-Legenden und Rāma-reliefs in Indonesien." [1]

The inequality of the sculptures, which is so noticeable at Borobudur, is even more marked in the Prambānam reliefs. Here and there are passages of great beauty of design and fine craftsmanship. But the imagination of the sculptors

[1] Georg Müller, Munich.

RÁMÁYANA RELIEF, PRAMBÁNAM, JAVA

often runs wild, in trying to depict the exploits of Rāma's monkey allies, and shows a tendency to incoherency in composition and looseness in technique.

Only a passing allusion can be made to the remarkable series of sculptures which adorn the great temple of Nakhon Vat, near Angkor, in Cambodia, a vast structure exceeding Borobudur in dimensions, the outer walled enclosure of it measuring two-thirds of a mile on each of its four sides. We are not, however, concerned with the magnificence of the architecture, details of which are given by Fergusson, but with the sculptures illustrating the Rāmāyana and Mahābhārata which decorate the walls of the temple. They are in very low relief, as they were not, like the Borobudur sculptures, intended for open-air effect, but for the reflected light of the magnificent colonnades under shelter of which they were placed. The whole of them, about six and a half feet in height and of an aggregate length of about two thousand feet, were originally gilt.

Casts of these fine sculptures are in the Ethnographic Museum, Berlin, and in the Trocadéro, Paris, but they are not displayed to great advantage there for lack of space. The most striking subject is the legend told in the Rāmāyana of the Churning of the Ocean by the gods and *asuras*, in order to procure *amrita*, the nectar of immortality. This is treated with immense

II

imaginative power and intensity of movement, but the sculptures as a rule do not possess the peculiar charm of Borobudur and Prambānam.

Most of the other subjects are battle scenes from the Mahābhārata, which are described with extreme elaboration and wonderful vigour. In the treatment of the human figure these Cambodia reliefs are strongly suggestive of the Amarāvatī sculptures.

In Cambodia, as in Java, many fine images of Indian origin have been found, for illustrations of which the reader must be referred to the publications of the École Française d'Extrême-Orient and other works dealing with that special subject.

We have now only to discuss the question of portraiture in Indian sculpture. From numerous references in Sanskrit literature it appears that painted portraiture was quite common in India in pre-Mogul times, but allusions to sculptured portraits, as distinguished from images of the gods, are rare. There are several in the Rāmā-yana ; one in which Rāma had an image made of Sītā. This was, however, only to meet the dilemma in which he was placed when, after Sītā's exile, he was advised to perform the great horse sacrifice, a ceremony which demanded the presence of his wife, as co-partner in religious rites. Rāma had a golden image of the Queen made for this occasion, and it was carried in front of the procession by his brother Bharat (*Uttara Kanda*, 25).

In two other instances Rāma's demon adversaries had life-like portraits made, but the context clearly shows that this branch of sculpture was considered to belong to the black rather than to the fine arts. The first was when Rāvana wanted to beguile his unhappy captive Sītā into believing that Rāma was dead. He ordered a skilful craftsman to make a life-like model of Rāma's head which was brought to Sītā, who,

" Seeing the severed head, and finding in the complexion of the face, in the eyes, in the hair, and in the jewelled knot, a likeness to her husband, and recognising it by all these signs and marks, became exceeding sad, and crying like a *kurari*, denounced Kaikeyi bitterly." — *Lanka Kanda*, 32.

In the same book, Indrajit, the son of Rāvana, had an image made of Sītā, and bringing it on his chariot in front of the contending armies, cut it down with his sword. The trick was so successful that even the astute Hanuman, Rāma's monkey ally, was deceived, and brought to Rāma the news of Sītā's death.

The word used in the text for a likeness— *māya*, illusion or deception—is significant of the orthodox Hindu attitude towards portraiture. It was the whole object of Hindu endeavour to get rid of *māya*, the illusive appearance of things, and to penetrate to the eternal Reality which stood behind it. For the artist to occupy himself with a simple imitation of nature was idle and impious. His aim must be to show the Divinity, which is the only reality. By the Hindu Shāstras, as well as by the law of Islam, statues of human beings, as such, are distinctly forbidden. In the Sukranitisāra, already alluded to,[1] it is said : " Only the images of the gods should be made, for they confer heaven and happiness ; but the images of men and others shut the door of heaven and bring ill-fortune." Again : " A misshapen image of God is always better than an image of man, however well made the latter may be." [2] This sufficiently explains why on old Indian coins we rarely find effigies of Hindu rulers. It also explains why, in Hindu sculpture, the tendency

[1] *Supra*, pp. 40–1.

[2] The same work, after the most minute instructions as to the correct proportions of images, from the total height down to the circumference of the thumb and great toe, adds the following explanations :

" In order that the form of an image may be brought out fully and clearly upon the mind, the image-maker must meditate, and his success will be in proportion to his meditation. No other way, not even seeing the object itself, will answer this purpose.

" To every part of the image should be given that grace and ease which is most suitable for it. . . . An image with a wrathful look should not have complacent eyes. Those images are handsome the measurements of which are in accordance with the rules of the Shāstras. Some, however, are of opinion that what pleases the heart is beautiful. But the measurements which do not agree with those given in the Shāstras cannot be pleasing to the cultured."

has always been to make representations of human beings, even when intended as portraiture, to conform to the ideal type of Divinity. It was impious to glorify man in his common personality, but not to explain him as one of the manifestations of the universal, divine nature. Europe says : " The noblest study of mankind is man " ; India declares it to be not man, but God, and Hindu art is only concerned in showing the relationship between the human and divine nature.

In the Buddhist period, however, this prejudice against ordinary portraiture was not so strong, and at Bhārhut and Sānchī there are sculptures of semi-divine beings showing a clearly marked individuality. One from Bhārhut is illustrated in Plate XXVIII. Among the later Gandhāran sculptures there are many strikingly characteristic heads which are so distinctly individual that they are taken by some archæologists to be portraits of Gandhāran kings ; but others consider them to be intended for Bodhisattvas, or for guardian demigods. Very likely they are idealised portraits of kings, deified after death as Bodhisattvas, according to the custom prevalent in Java and Cambodia.

Early Indian coinage also shows the most obvious portraiture ;[1] but this is pure Græco-Roman art, untouched by Indian influence. Evidently Græco-Roman artisans at one time had

[1] See frontispiece to Vincent Smith's " Early History of India."

almost a monopoly of some of the mints of northern India ; and this was, perhaps, the only craft in which Indians of that time were inferior to foreigners.

When the canons of Indian art were finally fixed as part of religious ritual, portraiture as a distinct branch of sculpture seems to have become almost extinct. In images of the gods the whole aim was to suggest a type of face as far as possible impersonal—that is, to suppress all the details indicative of human individuality, instead of creating a type of ideal human beauty, as in Greek art. Similarly at Borobudur we find human beings distinguished from one another, not as individuals, but as typical representatives of the class or caste to which they belong, chiefly by difference of dress, action, and gesture. But there is a great deal of Indian sculpture, especially in Java and Cambodia, in which a distinct ethnical type is taken for the head of a Buddha, Bodhisattva, or Hindu demigod, just as in the medieval art of Europe royal personages and dignitaries of the Church suggested the types of Christian saints.

In this, what we may call uncanonical Indian sculpture, we can find types of physiognomy and character given with the highest art, and with as much variety and power of expression as Greek sculpture can show, though it is not, strictly speaking, portraiture. Here Indian art comes

PLATE XLI

TWO HEADS OF BHIMA

into the same plane of thought as European, and
we can fairly draw a comparison between them.
That Indian sculptors did not attempt to portray
violent emotions and facial expression in the
same way as Europeans must again be attributed
to a difference of temperament and difference of
thought, not to want of capacity. Their religion
taught them that the way to spiritual advancement was by controlling human passions, and
this teaching strongly influenced their art. But
the common idea that Indian sculpture is lacking
in power of expression is just as wrong as other
uninformed opinions on Indian art. The best
Indian sculpture touched a deeper note of feeling
and finer sentiments than the best Greek.

Three ethnical types of extraordinary beauty
and character are given in Plates XLI and XLII.
According to popular tradition, which may or
may not be correct, the two on Plate XLI represent Bhima, one of the heroes of the Mahābhārata, famous for his strength and courage.
They are from an ancient Hindu temple, now
named after him locally, built in the plateau of
Dieng, Central Java. The third head, Plate
XLII, represents the Buddha himself. It also
comes from Java, but is now in the Leyden
Museum.

At first sight the suggestion they give of ancient
Egyptian or Greek art is almost startling. There
is the same greatness of line, broad generalisation,

and profound abstraction of the best Egyptian sculpture, and all the refinement of Greek art. But the similarity comes only from the kinship which exists between all truly great works of art, for these types are wholly Indian.

The contrast of the two characters is given with a depth of penetration which belongs only to the finest portraiture. In the two Bhima heads the artist, with a few bold clearly-drawn forms, shows us the born fighter and leader of men. In the large square forehead, the full firm jaws, the eyes set wide apart, and the determined mouth—half-savage, even cruel when his blood is roused—we recognise a young Alexander, a fighter who knows his strength and revels in it. All his desires are human, yet there is nothing low or brutal in his nature. He is a great national hero, a war-lord fit to lead and command a noble, free-born race.

Compare this with the head of the Buddha, Sākya-Muni. There is an infinity of difference in the type, yet the art is the same in its greatness and its inwardness. It is a true portrait-type of a high-bred intellectual Indian, but all that is pure, spiritual, and holy in Indian thought and religion is summed up in this supremely lovely face. The perfect oval shape, the small refined chin, and the finely chiselled features, speak of the god-like man who chose to leave all that was his—a royal throne, wealth, and earthly happiness

PLATE XLII

HEAD OF THE BUDDHA

—only to find the Way to help his suffering fellow-men.

The nobly vaulted brow and exquisitely formed eyes, with half-fallen meditative lids, tell us of infinite spiritual strength. A touch of sadness seems to rest on the full and tender lips, yet we can almost see them wreathed with a consoling, loving smile, and hear them utter words of blessing and perfect peace.

Compare it, if you will, with its assumed Gandhāran prototype, or with the Grecian models which Gandhāra had in its mind ; but there is in this art a depth and spirituality which never entered into the soul of Greece.

The method of treating the hair in formal curls, which is characteristic of the Indian ideal of the Buddha, has given rise to much archæological speculation and condemnation. The general conclusion, founded on the assumption of Indian artistic incapacity and bad taste, has been that Indian sculptors found the Grecian treatment, generally adopted in the Gandhāran sculptures, too difficult to imitate, and that in consequence they fell back upon this which Vincent Smith called " the feeble conventionalism of ordinary Indian art." [1]

If we adopt the alternative hypothesis that Indian artists possessed quite as much artistic

[1] " Journal of the Asiatic Society of Bengal," vol. lviii, 1889, p. 128.

sense as others, the explanation is not very far
to seek. In endeavouring to differentiate divine
beauty from that of mortals they look for those
characteristics which are uncommon in human
beings. To this day anything rare or abnormal
is popularly regarded in India as a special manifestation of the divine nature. Among Indians
of the highest castes, descended from the pure
Aryan stock, short curly hair is unusual, and held
as a sign of special distinction or good fortune.
Naturally enough, it was adopted by Indian
artists as one of the marks of divine beauty.

The formalism is only another Indian method of
showing that the divine nature transcends that
of common humanity. And when this conventionalism is thoroughly well carried out and
is a true expression of Indian thought there is no
justification for calling it " inartistic " or " de-
praved," except in the minds of those who are
convinced beyond argument that there is nothing
admirable in any art the ideals of which differ
from those of Greece and Italy.

Java and Cambodia are so rich in beautiful
types of sculpture of this class that volumes might
be filled with them. But we must now return to
India, the fountain-head, where the old art
traditions are still alive, whereas the art of Borobudur and Prambānam was practically extirpated
in Java by the conversion of the islanders to
Islam about the fifteenth century. The next

HORSE AND CHARIOTEER AT KANÂRAK

illustration, Plate XLIII, one of the grandest examples of Indian sculpture extant, not only shows the versatility of Indian sculptors in the past, but points to one of the many potential opportunities which might be opened to their descendants in the present day [1] if Anglo-Indians, instead of regarding them as ignorant children, would learn to make use of the extraordinary artistic resources of the land in which they live and rule. For certainly among all the commonplace statues of British Viceroys and Generals set up on the *maidans* of Calcutta and Bombay, there is not one to be placed in the same category as this. But as our own national craftsmanship has been practically exterminated we have only brought into India the bookman, the paper architect, and the eclectic or amateur artist, who find little beauty in Indian art and can do nothing with it but debase it.

Again, the thought occurs that had it by chance been labelled Roman or Greek, this magnificent work of art would now be the pride of some metropolitan museum in Europe or America. It is one of the two colossal war-horses adjoining the southern façade of the Kanārak temple in Orissa, said to have been built by Narasimha I, about the middle of the thirteenth century. The companion horse is completely mutilated, but

[1] The work of a traditional sculptor of the Orissa School now living is shown in Plate XXVII.

this one, apart from the broken ears and the missing head of the charioteer leading it, is almost intact, or was so not many years ago. Its surface, however, has suffered considerably from the weather, and from its exposed position it is likely to suffer more.

Visions of the Mahābhārata, of the clash of battle in heroic ages, and the memories of the past triumphs of Indian chivalry must have inspired the sculptor of this noble figure and his prancing, war-harnessed steed, pacing grandly forward over his prostrate foes. Here Indian sculptors have shown that they can express the pride of victory and the glory of triumphant warfare with as much fire and passion as the greatest European artists: for not even the Homeric grandeur of the Elgin Marbles surpasses the magnificent movement and modelling of this Indian Achilles, and the superbly monumental war-horse in its massive strength and vigour is not unworthy of comparison with Verocchio's famous masterpiece at Venice.

The art we see here is not the less great because there is a great deal in equine anatomy which this unknown sculptor has not cared to emphasise. As he had no modern dilettante critic to satisfy, he was free to make his statement of facts as simple and general as his artistic consciousness dictated, and to strike a note of epic grandeur hardly ever heard in any modern art.

PLATE XLIV

KUVERA
(From Nepāl.)

The next illustration, Plate XLIV, is of a very different type, and belongs to another school. It is a copper-gilt statuette from Nepāl, now in the Calcutta Art Gallery, representing a demigod, probably Kuvera, the god of worldly prosperity. Divested of his divine attributes, the crown and two supplementary arms, it is a vivid and speaking portrait of a well-fed, self-indulgent Lama or Brahman priest, fond of good living and of all things which make life easy and comfortable.

The contrast between this very mundane deity and the idealised spiritual type we have seen before is very striking. Here the artist has only wanted to show the human body without the divine soul, and in this animated and strongly modelled figure it is evident that he is as capable of doing this as any European sculptor.

It is thoroughly modern and European in all its sentiment. There are no dreams, no religious ecstasy, no high spiritual ideals. It is a personification of materialism and the worldly life. The movement of the fingers speaks of prayer, but the prayers are for worldly, not spiritual benefits. The coarse, strong features and very lively expression of the face indicate sensuality and intellectual power of a low, self-seeking kind, combined with an infinite capacity for the enjoyment of the pleasures of life. The body, well-fed and rounded in every limb, makes it clear that hard work and abstinence is not part of the gospel

he preaches. European artists who have neither
the time nor the opportunity to study Eastern
art commonly assert that the oriental can neither
draw nor model the human figure correctly,
although oriental life gives far better opportunities
for the study of the nude than the artist has in
Europe. The criticism is as superficial as it is
unjust. The Eastern artist, like the Western,
draws what he wants to draw and models what he
wants to model. The failure of the European
to understand oriental draughtsmanship comes
either from his inability, or from his unwillingness,
to understand the intention of it.

I will conclude this brief study of Indian portrait sculpture with another example of the
Nepalese School, a copper-gilt statuette of a
Tibetan nun, or abbess, holding the usual
sacerdotal drum, made of human skulls, in the
right hand, and a beggar's bowl in the left
(Plate XLV). The original, like the last example,
belongs to the collection which the author made
for the Calcutta Art Gallery.

This is another delightfully conceived and
admirably executed portrait study of an ordinary
human being. The real type the artist knew was,
perhaps, a frowsy, unkempt, ugly, and awkward
Tibetan woman, mumbling an empty formula,
with a dull monotonous drum-beat as an accompaniment. But guided unconsciously by his inherited art-traditions, and without any desire to

PLATE XLV

A TIBETAN NUN

flatter or idealise, he has succeeded in expressing, in the whole attitude and in the treatment of the dress and all the accessories, that style and dignity which national feeling and respect for the spiritual calling of his subject demanded, even though individuals should be found unworthy of it. In all these portrait types, reflecting so sincerely and truthfully the soul of the people, we can feel the different outlook of a great hereditary artistic tradition, compared with that of the petty individualistic art of modern Europe, with all its narrowness, self-consciousness, and provincialism. "Whole æras," said Ruskin, "of mighty history are summed and the passions of dead myriads are concentrated in the existence of a noble (national) art; and if that art were among us we should feel it and rejoice."

We Europeans who live in India to-day have such an art still living amongst us; but the history is not our history. The passions of those dead myriads do not move us. So we neither feel it nor rejoice, but rather trample it heedlessly under our feet.

PART II

PAINTING

CHAPTER I

INDIAN MURAL PAINTING

THE building of New Delhi has not, apparently, provided any opportunities for Indian painters, but it has drawn attention to the subject of mural painting, now reckoned, like architecture, among the lost, or forgotten arts of India.

As in other countries the art of painting in India became a potent force in national culture in the great schools of mural decoration, and gradually lost touch with real life when pictures came to be regarded more as articles of luxury for the connoisseur than as a means of instruction and spiritual uplift for the whole community.

It is evident from early Buddhist records how closely painting was associated with popular festivals and with civic life in ancient India. No town or village festival was complete unless the streets were made gay with pictures painted on the house-fronts or on scrolls and banners hung on temporary screens of bambu. The traditions of this folk-art are still alive.

While painted stone or wood-carving gradually

155

superseded mural painting in the great temples and stūpas, built to last for ages, painting of the highest class held its own in the *chitra-sālas* of kings' palaces, which were more or less of a temporary character. A *chitra-sāla*, or gallery of mural paintings, was an indispensable annexe to a Hindu palace until quite modern times, or until Indian art fell into disrepute and it became fashionable for Indian princes to import inferior European oil-paintings and European furniture.

The process employed was usually that which is known in Italy as *fresco buono*, in which colours mixed with lime-water are applied to a prepared surface of the finest plaster, while it is still wet, so that they are chemically united with the ground. Indian *fresco buono*, when the wall is a suitable one, is an exceedingly permanent process for interior decoration, and much more durable in a tropical climate than oil-painting. But as it was largely used in exposed situations or in buildings which were not in themselves of a permanent kind, very few of the early Indian fresco-paintings have survived.

These palatial *chitra-sālas* were quadrangular cloisters surrounding one of the palace gardens or pavilions, sometimes reserved for the ladies of the zanana and sometimes apparently a public resort. There are many allusions to them in Sanskrit literature. The Rāmāyana describes Rāvana's palace in Ceylon, where

Gay, blooming creepers clothed the walls,
Green bowers were there and picture-halls,
And chambers made for soft delight.[1]

But the most detailed and interesting description of them is given by Bhavabhuti, the great dramatist of the sixth century, in his "Uttara Rāma Charita," translated by Wilson. Here a whole scene in the first act is devoted to an animated description of a series of pictures illustrating the Rāmāyana, like the reliefs sculptured in the courtyard of the Siva temple at Prambānam described above. The *dramatis personæ* are Rāma, king of Ayodhyā, Sītā, his queen, and Lakshman his brother and faithful companion in exile.

Lakshman invites Rāma to come and look at the pictures :

Come, my most noble brother, on these walls
Behold a skilful artist has portrayed
Your story as he learnt it late from me.

The next scene, called " the contemplation of the picture," is laid in a pavilion in the garden of the palace. The walls on which the pictures were painted were those which enclosed the garden and pavilion.

Enter LAKSHMANA, SĪTĀ, *and* RĀMA

LAKSH.   Behold the picture.
SĪTĀ.   What are these that crowd
Around my lord, and seem to hymn his praises ?

[1] " Sunda Kanda," Griffiths' trans., Book V, Cant. VI, p. 297.

LAKSH. These are the heavenly arms,[1] that Vishvamitra,
    The holy sage from Kusa sprung, the friend
    Of all mankind, obtained from great Krisawa,
    And gave them to the prince to wage the fight
    With that malignant demon Taraka.

The next panel of the painting showed Rāma when as a youth he competed for the hand of Sītā at the court of her father, Janaka, king of Videha, breaking the famous bow of Siva which no other suitor had been able to bend.

Sītā herself describes the picture :

    Yes, I see my lord.
    Dark as the deep blue lotus is his hue,
    And strength and grace in every limb appear,
    Paternal looks dwell wondering on his face,
    Lovely with graceful curls, whilst high disdain
    Swells every feature, as with force divine
    He snaps asunder the celestial bow.

The relief at Borobudur, illustrating the similar episode in the legendary life of the Buddha (Plate XXXVI), will give us a suggestion of this painting.

The next panel depicted the marriage of Rāma and Sītā and those of his three brothers :

    SĪTĀ. A solemn scene, where gifts of kine secure
    Auspicious destiny, and four bright youths
    Are knit in marriage bonds with four fair maids ;
    I recognise you all—and there, and there am I.

[1] The arms with which Rāma fought against his demon adversaries, personified.

Farther along the wall Rāma recognises the picture of his bride when he brought her back to his father's palace at Ayodhyā, before the cruel decree of banishment drove them both to the seclusion of the forest :

> RĀMA.   Ah, too well,
> Too well does memory bring back the time
> When yet an honoured sire was alive,
> Whilst yet a mother's love watched o'er our being ;
> When all was joy.   Ah me, those days are gone !
> But here behold—see how the youthful bride,
> Fair Sītā, wins maternal admiration ;
> Her smiling countenance resplendent shines
> With youth and loveliness ; her lips disclose
> Teeth white as jasmine buds ; her silky curls
> Luxuriant shade her cheeks, and every limb
> Of brightest texture moves with natural grace,
> Like moonbeams gliding through the yielding air.

The dramatist skilfully indicates the varied emotions of the royal spectators, as they review all the incidents of their past life depicted on the walls—their happiness in the jungle hut on the banks of the Godavery :

> RĀMA.   Recall'st thou, love, our humble happy dwelling,
> Upon the borders of the shining stream,
> Where every hour in fond endearment wrapped,
> Or in the sweet interchange of thought engaged,
> We lived in transport, not a wish beyond
> Each other, reckless of the flight of time ?

Their encounter with the demons, the abduction of Sītā and the distracted grief of Rāma, the

devotion of the eagle-king, Jatayu, killed by
Rāvana while desperately struggling to rescue
Sītā ; the valour of Rāma's monkey allies, and
the heroic deeds by which the demon's stronghold
in Ceylon was at last captured and Sītā's release
effected, were all depicted on the walls of Rāma's
chitra-sāla.

In classical Sanskrit literature painting is considered an occupation not unworthy of princes.
In the Nāgānanda, a drama attributed to King
Harsha of Kanauj (606–47), a prince of the
Vidhyādharas whiles away his time by drawing
the portrait of his beloved, Malayāvatī. He asks
for a piece of red arsenic to draw with and his
attendant picks up from the ground pieces of
clay or stone of five different colours—blue,
yellow, red, brown, and grey. Malayāvatī unobserved watches her lover at work, but the
portrait is so indifferent that she believes it is
intended for some other fair maid and faints away
from jealousy.

There are so many references to painted portraits in Sanskrit literature that evidently the
prohibition in the Silpā-śāstras applied only
to temples and other sacred buildings and
not to the practice of painting as a secular
accomplishment.

In a play attributed to Kālidāsa the heroine
is the Queen Dhārinī's beautiful attendant, Mālavikā, who is a skilful musician and dancer. The

Queen carefully keeps her attractive handmaid
from the presence of the King, Agnimitra, but
foolishly caused Mālavikā's portrait to be
painted on the walls of the *chitra-sāla*. The
plot of the play discloses the disastrous con-
sequences of the King's next visit to the picture
gallery.

In Kālidāsa's famous play, Sakuntala, a considerable part of Act VI is taken up with a
painted portrait of the Queen, with which the
King Dushyanta, half-demented with grief and
remorse for his desertion of Sakuntala, attempts
to console himself. In the text translated by
Sir William Jones, this portrait is said to be
painted by a lady of the Court, but the more
recent version of Monier-Williams makes the
king himself the artist.

The picture represented Sakuntala and her two
attendants in the garden of the hermitage where
Dushyanta first saw them. Sakuntala herself
is leaning " apparently a little tired against the
stem of a mango-tree, the tender leaves of which
glitter with the water she has poured upon them.
Her arms are gracefully extended ; her face is
somewhat flushed with the heat, and a few
flowers have escaped from her hair, which has
become unfastened and hangs in loose tresses
about her neck."

The king, looking at the picture, declares that
the background is unfinished and sends an

attendant to fetch the painting implements.
He will have the River Mālinī portrayed in it :

> Its tranquil course by banks of sand impeded,
> Upon the brink a pair of swans ; beyond,
> The hills adjacent to Himalaya,
> Studded with deer ; and near the spreading shade
> Of some large tree, where 'mid the branches hang
> The hermits' vests of bark, a tender doe,
> Rubbing its downy forehead on the horn
> Of a black antelope, should be depicted.

Then he would add some ornaments to the
figure of Sakuntala :

> A sweet Sirisha blossom should be twined
> Behind the ear ; its perfumed crest depending
> Towards her cheek ; and resting on her bosom,
> A lotus-fibre necklace, soft and bright
> As an autumnal moonbeam.

His companion, Māthavya, notices that Sakuntala is covering her lips with one hand as if to
prevent a bee, which " intent on thieving honey
from the flowers seems to have mistaken her
mouth for a rosebud," from settling on her lips.
This was an incident which had actually occurred
at the King's first meeting with Sakuntala, as
described in the first act, and Dushyanta, led on
by the vividness of the painting to imagine that it
was reality, calls out :

" A bee ! drive off the impudent insect, will
you ? "

The story will recall similar ones recorded of

ancient Greek artists and their skill in imitative
painting. A very similar one is told of the first
Chinese painter known in history, Tsao Fuh-king,
the court painter to the Emperor Sun K'uan, in
the third century A.D. In this case a fly was so
skilfully imitated that the Emperor raised his
hand to brush it off.[1]

Both of Kālidāsa's translators use the word
" canvas " in describing the picture. Some of the
old Central Asian paintings discovered by Dr.
von Lecoq are painted on cloth prepared with a
ground of lime like some modern Tibetan paintings, so it is not unlikely that a canvas of this
kind was used by Indian painters in the time of
Kālidāsa. But from the Sanskrit text it would
appear more probable that a wooden panel is
intended.

Of this secular art of painting of pre-Muhammadan times there are no Indian examples
extant, but from what we know of the religious
sculpture and of the technical excellence of the
best paintings of the Ajantā School we can fairly
assume that the merit ascribed to it by Sanskrit
writers was not overrated.

The period covered by the Ajantā paintings is
supposed to extend over some six centuries, or
from about the second to the seventh century
A.D. Though these wonderful viharas when they
were inhabited must have been extraordinarily

[1] Anderson, " Pictorial Arts of Japan."

beautiful, it must not be supposed that the object of the paintings was to provide entertainment for, or to gratify the æsthetic tastes of, the Buddhist monks—the walls were the picture-books used for instructing the pilgrims and novices of the Order in the events of the Buddha's many existences. If sometimes the subjects seem to be out of keeping with the ascetic life of a monastery, it is only because the Master had experienced life in every phase before he reached Nirvāna, the perfect experience. And though incidentally the pictures give an intimate revelation of Indian life of the period, it would be a mistake to suppose that the painters intentionally recorded current events as history.

As works of art the Ajantā paintings, like the Borobudur reliefs, are of unequal merit, though some are worthy to rank among the great pictures of the world.

It is often said that Indian painting is to be distinguished from that of the West as being an art of line only, that is Indian paintings are not true pictures in the European sense, they are only coloured drawings. This is true of the earlier and of most of the later schools of Indian painting. But it is not true of the grand school of Indian mural painting, in the highest development it reached at Ajantā, Bagh, Sigiri, and in the recently discovered Pallava paintings at Sittannavāsal.

In the great flowering time of Buddhist-Hindu art, from Gupta times down to the Muhammadan invasions, there was a marked tendency to prefer painted reliefs to simple fresco and tempera paintings for the decoration of temple walls ; though the painters' share in the work was an important one, for without the eye-painting ceremony with its appropriate mantras a stone image was not " alive," or filled with the Divine Presence, and could not, therefore, be worshipped. The combination of sculpture and painting, often practised as a single craft, was the highest form of religious art, being more difficult and costly than simple painting, and therefore conferring more merit both on the artist-devotees and their patrons.

The religious sentiment had its natural re-action on the practice of fresco and tempera painters. They tried to imitate plastic effects ; not to produce the atmosphere of Western paint-ing, but to give their work the solidity and reality of sculpture. The classic examples of Indian pictorial art, therefore, show something more than an art of line. These Indian painters did indeed rival the best Chinese masters in their wonderful power of delineation, but they also excelled in the subtle modelling of surfaces. Whether they were modelled by the painter or the sculptor, the finishing brush-outline gave life to the forms.

Writing on the technique of the Ajantā paintings Mr. J. Griffiths says :

" The artists who painted them were giants in execution. Even on the vertical sides of the walls some of the lines which were drawn by one sweep of the brush struck me as being very wonderful ; but when I saw long delicate curves drawn without faltering, with equal precision, upon the horizontal surface of a ceiling, where the difficulty of execution is increased a thousand-fold, it appeared to me nothing less than miraculous. One of the students, when hoisted up on the scaffolding, tracing his first panel on the ceiling, naturally remarked that some of the work looked like child's work, little thinking that what seemed to him, up there, rough and meaningless, had been laid on with a cunning hand, so that when seen at its right distance every touch fell into its proper place." [1]

A great deal of misconception of the true character of these paintings is due to the fact that nearly all the published material for the study of them has been derived from copies, carefully traced by hand, which give a very faint impression of the marvellous beauty and freedom of the brush-outlines, the masterly plastic treatment of the surfaces, and the exquisite delicacy and refinement of ornamental details. These copies, made under great difficulties, are by no means to

[1] " Indian Antiquary," vol. iii, 1874, p. 26.

PLATE XLVI

THE BUDDHA'S RETURN TO HIS HOME

(Painting in Antechamber, Cave XVII, Ajantā)

SKETCH SHOWING THE FULL DESIGN AND
PROPORTIONS OF THE PAINTING, "THE
RETURN OF THE BUDDHA"

be depreciated. They are most useful records of the general design, and in some cases supply details which cannot be distinguished by the camera. But it cannot be too strongly insisted that hand-copies must be supplemented by the best reproductions which scientific photography can make. For artists and art-students a first-rate photograph is infinitely more valuable than the best hand-copy.

For the first edition of this book the only materials available were the copies made by the students of the Bombay School of Art, published by Mr. Griffiths in his work on Ajantā, and these furnished the only illustration given of the Ajantā School, a very inadequate and incomplete copy of the wonderful painting in the antechamber of Cave XVII, undoubtedly the greatest achievement of the school. The same group, inexplicably divorced from its context, was illustrated in Lady Herringham's work. A complete, but not quite accurate copy, showing the colour-scheme and the whole design, was subsequently made by Mr. Mukul Chandra Dey and published by him in his " Pilgrimages to Ajantā and Bagh."[1]

The long wanted photographic survey of the paintings, commenced by M. Victor Goloubeff in 1911, is now being completed by the Archæological Survey of Hyderabad, and through the

[1] The copy is now in the Oriental Department of the British Museum.

kindness of the Director, Mr. G. Yazdani, I am
enabled to give more satisfactory reproductions
of the painting (Plates XLVI–VII and Pl. XLVIA)
of which a very discerning critic, Mr. Binyon,
has said that no picture anywhere is more impressive in grandeur and tenderness.

Though the unknown Ajantā artist has not
followed strictly the authorised version of the
legend, there can be no doubt as to the subject
of the painting.[1] It is the legend of the return
of the Buddha to his home, after the Enlightenment. One spring morning, eight months after
he had attained Buddhahood, the Blessed One
resolved to revisit his native city, Kapilavastu.
Travelling on foot and begging his food from door
to door, as was the custom of all the Buddhas,
he reached the city after a two-months' journey.
The Sākya princes, his former companions, went
out with flowers in their hands to greet him and
led him to a pleasant grove in the outskirts of the
city. But, regarding him as a younger brother,
they would not do obeisance to him until he
assumed his Divine Form and rising into the air
filled the whole universe with his Presence,
performing many miracles which made the King,
his father, and all his courtiers fall down in worship.

[1] A very inferior painting of the same subject in Cave XIX is
illustrated in Griffiths' " Ajantā " (Plate 89, Fig. 5) and in Vincent
Smith's " History of Fine Art in India and Ceylon," Fig. 208.

PLATE XLVII

YASODHARĀ AND RĀHULA

The next day the Buddha went into the city to beg for alms. Lotus-flowers sprang up beneath his feet, a glory shone round his head, and he comes at last to the door of his own palace presenting his begging bowl. Yasodharā, his wife, leading Rāhula, now seven years old, comes out and worships him, saying, " O Siddhartha, that night Rāhula was born you rejected your kingdom and went silently away. Now you have a more glorious kingdom instead ! "

The wall-space chosen by the artist lends itself admirably to the noble design of the picture. It is a narrow upright panel at one end of the antechamber, framed on the right-hand side by the richly carved architrave of the doorway leading into the shrine. The palace walls are cunningly made to abut on to the architrave of the doorway, leaving a narrow upright space filled by the majestic figure of the glorified Buddha towering over the palace roof. A Vidhyādhara, flying over the Buddha's head and holding over it a flower-decked umbrella, fills the upper part of the panel which is narrowed again by the projecting lintel of the doorway.

Yasodharā, wearing on this day of gladness the jewellery she has discarded for seven long desolate years, stands at her door, gazing up in adoration at the glorious apparition in front of her and holding out caressingly the precious gift she offers to the Divine Beggar, her darling

13

child. The Buddha, graciously bending his head, accepts Rāhula as his disciple.

The artist has indeed been wonderfully inspired, in the grand spacing out of the whole design, in his conception of the Divine Form, majestic in its simple and austere lines, and in the tenderness and pathos he has given to the figures of the mother and child, drawn in rhythmic brush-lines with exquisite delicacy and charm (Plate XLVII).

Like all the Ajantā paintings, this masterpiece has suffered irremediable damage, the lower portion having been almost completely destroyed. But the entire spacing out of the panel and the true proportions of it can be seen in Pl. XLVIA. The photographic reproduction, Plate XLVI, unfortunately has stunted the proportions of the Buddha by omitting both the lower part of the panel, where a portion of the lotus-flower springing under his feet is to be seen, and also the blackened upper part filled by the umbrella.

It is very much to be desired that all the resources of scientific photography may be applied to the task of making the best possible record of this great painting and others which have not yet been worthily reproduced. Such reproductions, enlarged to full size, might provide material for an " Ajantā Museum," worthy of India, designed to give a complete replica of two or three of these magnificent monastic halls, and to demonstrate the perfect co-ordination of building

PLATE XLVIII

HEAD OF BODHISATTVA

(From a Painting in Cave I, Ajantā)

design, sculpture, and painting into a higher organic unity, which, as Professor Lethaby has said, is the true test of noble architecture. Thus India might hand down to posterity a complete record of the golden age of her art, and help to revive the grand traditions of her own school of mural painting, not yet extinct.

The lovely head of the Bodhisattva in Cave I, Plate XLVIII, from a photograph kindly provided by M. Goloubeff, will give, in spite of its damaged condition, a good impression of the broad plastic treatment of the later Ajantā paintings. The brush-outlines here visible are not the foundation of the painting, but the finishing touches which give emphasis and reality to the surface modelling.

There has been much discussion regarding the exact process used by the painters of Ajantā and Bagh, and much difference of opinion among experts. Sir John Marshall says that it is tempera painting, not *fresco buono*. There cannot be any doubt, however, that the true fresco process has been practised in India for many centuries. It was used by Akbar's painters in the decoration of Fatehpur-Sikri, and is still used by the temple craftsmen of Rajputana, or was so about twenty years ago, when I engaged a Jaipur painter to decorate the entrance hall of the Calcutta School of Art and to give instruction to the students. The process is described in the Appendix. Plate XLIX shows part of the wall decoration of the school executed throughout in *fresco buono*, and Plate LXXII a fresco panel painted at the same time by Dr. Abanindra Nath Tagore, C.I.E. No attempt was made to imitate the technique or style of the Ajantā school, but simply to open a door for the revival of art in India which departmentalism has long kept shut.

It cannot be supposed that the process was introduced into India by the Moguls, and one would certainly expect to find it used by the earlier schools of Indian mural painting. As a matter of fact the *intonaco*, the thin plaster ground at Ajantā, Bagh, and elsewhere, is exactly the same as that used by the Rajput temple craftsmen at the present day. M. Goloubeff, in his admirable monograph on Ajantā,[1] says that the paintings are true frescoes, though some of them have been finished or retouched by a process analogous to tempera. In other words the Ajantā paintings seem to be a combination of *fresco buono* and *fresco secco*. This view is supported by very good historical evidence, the hereditary craft-tradition of Indian mural painting.

It is hardly necessary now, as it was twenty years ago, to insist that the Ajantā School is purely Indian and not, as Dr. Vincent Smith maintained, " a local development of the cosmopolitan art of the contemporary Roman Empire." The painting in Cave I, described by him as a " vivid

[1] " Ars Asiatica," vol. x.

PLATE XLIX

MODERN MURAL DECORATION IN INDIAN *FRESCO BUONO*

representation of the ceremonial attending the presentation of their credentials by the Persian Envoys " (from Khushru II of Persia to Pulikesin of Mahārāshtra, in the thirty-sixth year of his reign, A.D. 625–6), and cited as a signal proof of the derivative character of the Ajantā School, has been shown by M. Foucher to be no historical painting, " a landmark in the history of art," but an illustration of a jātaka story, like most of the other paintings in the Caves.

The discovery in 1920 of fresco paintings in a rock-cut temple at Sittannavāsal in the ancient Pallava country, not far from Pudukkottai, through the brilliant archæological researches conducted by Professor Jouveau-Dubreuil, has added an important chapter to the history of the great school of Indian mural painting. Mr. N. C. Mehta, I.C.S., in his " Notes on Indian Paintings," [1] has published coloured sketches of some of them, but the scientific photographic survey necessary for the full appreciation of their artistic value has yet to be made.

They are attributed by Professor Jouveau-Dubreuil to the reign of Mahendravarman I, *circ.* A.D. 600–25, one of the great Pallava dynasty which dominated the south for two centuries and gave to Indian art the wonderful sculptures of Māmallapuram. They therefore seem to be contemporary with the finest paintings of Ajantā.

[1] Taraporeavala Sons & Co., Bombay.

The principal subject, says Professor Jouveau-Dubreuil, is a grand fresco which adorns the whole of the ceiling of the verandah, representing a lotus tank enlivened with fish, geese, buffaloes, elephants, and three human or divine figures, devotees or Gandharvas, holding in their hands the lotus flowers and leaves they are gathering. On two of the pillars of the façade are two paintings of Devadāsis dancing the dance of Siva. Unfortunately the photographs of these most impressive fragments which I have been able to secure, though they prove them to be the work of a great artist, are not suitable for reproduction. But Plate L, for which I am indebted to the kind help of Mr. S. V. Ramasami Mudeliar of Madras, will indicate that the painters of Sittannavāsal were in no way inferior to the best of the Pallava sculptors. The youth whose graceful figure makes rhythmic play with the lotus leaves and flowers is drawn with all the power and freedom of the classical Indian school at its best. It is interesting to note that the design has been put on the wall or ceiling in the first instance by stencilling, the dots of the pouncing being clearly visible under the vigorous strokes of the finishing brushwork. In the Sittannavāsal frescoes also the different quality of the master-painter's work and that of his assistants or apprentices, can be clearly distinguished in different parts of the decorative scheme. Plate L

PLATE L

FRESCO AT SITTANNAVĀSAL

undoubtedly shows the hand of the master
himself.

Ceylon, which is very rich in sculptured monuments of Indian origin, also furnishes some remarkable remains of mural paintings, well worth
a separate monograph, apparently derived from
the great school of Ajantā. They are situated in
two caves excavated on the western face of the
wonderful Sigiri rock in the central province of
the island, and it has been assumed that they are
the work of the court painters of the parricide
King Kāsyapa I (A.D. 479–497), who made this
impregnable rock his stronghold, and that they
represent his queens with their attendants going
to worship at the neighbouring Buddhist monastery. No satisfactory explanation has been given
of the reason why the queens and their handmaidens appear as if half immersed in clouds,
the usual convention of the heavenly spheres.
The suggestion that this was merely a device to
make up for the cramped space which the painters
had to fill is very unconvincing. But if we
imagine that one of the royal ladies dreamed
of a visit to the Tusita heavens, and that the
court painters, or those attached to the monastery, took this for their subject as an everyday
event in Buddhist religious life, the difficulty
would be removed.

Fortunately a complete photographic record of
the paintings, which owing to their inaccessible

position have been much better preserved than those of Ajantā and Bagh, has been made by the Archæological Survey of Ceylon. There are twenty-one figures in all, three of which are shown in Plate LI. As usual, some of them are by the hand of a master-painter and others by the pupils working with him ; this was the way the master passed on the torch his ancestors had lighted for him to the next generation. The monuments we guard to-day as archæological treasures served the purpose of modern art galleries and schools of art.

There is a peculiar charm about these Sigiri paintings in the expression of the wonder and delight felt by the visitors to the celestial spheres, in the grace and spontaneity of movement, quite free from any academic pose, and in the strength and vitality of the drawing and modelling.

The Bagh rock-cut viharas, in the Gwalior State, contain some of the most important remains of the grand school of Indian painting, in its best period, about the seventh century A.D. A good set of copies of the principal frescoes, made for the Gwalior Durbar, a duplicate of which is in the British Museum, gave the material for a recent publication by the India Society, but the indispensable photographic survey has not yet been made and it is improbable that any measures taken for the preservation of the paintings *in situ*

PLATE LI

TWO PAINTINGS FROM SIGIRI, CEYLON

A GROUP FROM THE GREAT FRESCO OF THE RANG MAHALL, BAGH

176]

will stop the progress of the rapid decay which has already destroyed the greater part of them. Indian art will surely suffer further irreparable loss unless these precious fragments are removed from the walls of the viharas and placed under proper care in a suitable museum or art gallery.

The sympathetic copy of the fascinating group of dancers and musicians, Plate LII, made by Mr. Asit Kumar Haldar in a limited time under considerable difficulties, gives a good impression of the life and movement of one of the most attractive passages in the great fresco of the Rang Mahall, Cave IV, though only a photograph can reproduce the consummate technique of the brush-lines and the surface modelling. The subject, a group of girl musicians gathered in a ring round two male dancers, suggests a variation of the Indian artist's central theme—the universal Dance of Siva. The rhythmic curves of their vividly striped dresses give the impression of a band of nereids sporting in a sea of music, keeping time with the ripple of the waves.

This, however, is only an incident in the main subject of the fresco, a great procession of horsemen and elephant riders sweeping across the wall in a stately city pageant, representing undoubtedly, not a contemporary event, but some familiar tale told by the monks for the edification of the pilgrim visitors.

The technical tradition of the great school of

Indian mural painting survives, as we have seen, in the temple craftsmanship of the present day in Rajputana. The Ajantā tradition was also brought down to modern times in the numerous paintings and drawings, mostly by Rajput and Kangra artists, illustrating in miniature Vaishnava and Saiva myths and legends as they were depicted formerly on the walls of Hindu *chitra-sālas*. Plate LIII, " The Birth Ceremony of the Infant Krishna," a brush drawing of the Kangra School, carefully shaded to give an impression of relief, puts the Krishna legend in a modern Rajput setting, but preserves the spirit which informed the great art of Ajantā and very much of its technique.

The painted icons used in Vaishnava household worship formed another link, now almost broken, which connected classical Indian art with modern times. A very interesting example, probably of the eighteenth century, Plate LIV, represents in iconographical form the Coronation of Rāma and Sītā at Ayodhyā after the overthrow of Rāvana and the termination of their exile. Rāma's sword and the famous bow of Siva are on the ground in front of him ; Hanuman the monkey-king, his faithful ally, kneels and clasps the King's leg. His three brothers are in attendance on Rāma's right hand ; on the opposite side a bevy of court ladies and musicians wait on the Queen. The details of the throne, the royal crowns,

THE BIRTH CEREMONY OF THE INFANT KRISHNA

and the umbrella are rendered in relief with gilt gesso and glass. Real pearls are used in the ornaments. In the background is given a realistic picture of the palace and citadel of Ayodhyā, with its inhabitants; courtiers, men-at-arms, richly caparisoned elephants and war-horses; the temples and sacred cows, the public bathing tank, the city walls, the river, and the country beyond—a perfect microcosm of the life and ceremonial of a royal Indian city.

The still living Tibetan school of painting and sculpture is an offshoot of Nepalese Buddhist art dating from the time of King Srong-tsan-gampo in the seventh century A.D. The crafts-men of the Tibetan monasteries, painters and sculptors, cling tenaciously to the old traditions, and much might be learnt from them, though it is in technique rather than in spiritual outlook that they stand in close relation with the art of India. Tibet is part of the hinterland of Indian art, half-way between India and China, which can only be dealt with satisfactorily in a comprehen-sive monograph, but a few suggestions on colour symbolism which Tibetan artists borrowed from Buddhist India may be noted :

The Manikabum, a Tibetan work of the seventh century, gives the symbolic colours appropriate for each of the six syllables of the famous Sanskrit Mantra Aum Mani Padme Hum, which is said to save from rebirth in either of the six conditions, i.e. as a *deva, asura,* man, animal, goblin or hopeless being, or as a devil.

The colour of AUM, the heavenly state, is white. White, both in Buddhist and orthodox Hindu symbolism, signifies heavenly purity and bliss. It is a symbol of Siva and of his snow-clad paradise, and also of Parvati, his consort. It may also represent water.

The colour of MA, the *asura* state, is blue. In Hindu orthodoxy blue is the colour of Vishnu, the Preserver, and of his incarnations, Krishna and Rāma.

The colour of NI, the human state, is yellow, like the ascetic's robe.

Images of Buddha, as well as those of Maitreya and Manjusri, are painted a golden yellow. It is also the symbol of earth.

The colour of PAD, the animal state, is green, while that of ME, the state of a hopeless being or goblin, is red. This is in direct opposition to Brahmanical symbolism, in which red is the colour of the sun-god, Sūrya, of the solar sphere, the abode of spirits whose earthly migrations are finished, and also of Brahmā, the Creator. King Harsha's father is said to have offered daily to Sūrya a bunch of red lotus-flowers, in a vessel of ruby red.

The colour of HUM, the state of a devil, is black.

But in the Hindu Sāstras black symbolises the formless unconditioned state which existed

THE CORONATION OF RÁMA AND SÍTÁ

before Creation, personified by Kālī, the Mother of the Universe and the Great Destroyer. The Nirvāna Tantra says, " As the lightning is born from the cloud and disappears within the cloud, so Brahmā and all the gods take birth from Kālī and disappear in Kālī."

The three *gunas*, or qualities of Matter, have their colour symbols — *sattvam*, white ; *rajas*, yellow or red ; *tamas*, blue or black.

According to the Vishnudharmottaram,[1] a Sanskrit treatise on painting, the colouring of things seen should be true to nature, but the colouring of images and also that of a certain category of pictures descriptive of the *rasas*, or emotions, must be according to the rules of symbolism. Every *rasa* had its appropriate colour : the emotion of love, dark blue ; of laughter, white ; of compassion, grey ; of rage, red ; of valour or heroism, yellowish white ; of terror, black ; of astonishment or feeling of the supernatural, yellow ; and of loathing, indigo blue.

The specialised schools of painting mentioned above, which were developed as part of the culture of the Buddhist or Hindu monastery, temple, or court, grew up from a broad substratum of popular pictorial art, some of it very primitive, some of it, like the " Pat " drawings of Bengal described by Mr. Asit Ghose,[2] showing a technical

[1] See Dr. Stella Kramrisch's translation, pp. 16–17.
[2] " Indian Art and Letters," vol. ii, No. 2, 1926.

skill of a high order. From very early times this substratum served as a means of religious propaganda among the illiterate masses. In the Sārattha-Pakasini, says Dr. Kramrisch, allusion is made to a class of Brahmans known by the name of Nakha, who wandered about with pictures mounted on a portable framework, showing " scenes of good and evil destinies, of fortunes and misfortunes," and pointing out that " by doing this deed one attains this, and by doing that one attains that." The moral and religious teaching of the great Hindu epics was, and still is to a certain extent, popularised in a similar way by minstrel-painters wandering from village to village, but the scheme of modern progress elaborated by the educated townsman has no use for this traditional method of popular culture, so the Indian villager desirous of recreation or edification must wait patiently until the cinema points the modern way to spiritual enlightenment, or prostitution.

CHAPTER II

PAINTING IN MOGUL TIMES

WE have seen in the last chapter that in the pre-Muhammadan period the art of painting was cultivated as a dilettante amusement or accomplishment in the courts of Buddhist and Hindu sovereigns, but it was not until Mogul times that a distinctly secular school of painting, derived originally from Persia, arose in India. This secularisation of art in the Mogul period in India may be compared with the Renaissance in Europe.

The direct origin of this secularisation was the formal prohibition by the Muhammadan law of the representation of animate nature in art. The effect of this law was virtually to suppress the practice of painting and sculpture as fine arts in all countries under Muhammadan rule, from the founding of the Caliphate of Baghdad down to the beginning of the thirteenth century.

With the decline of the spiritual power of the Caliphs the prohibition ceased to have full effect, but the revival of pictorial art in Persia did not really begin until the overthrow of Arab rule by the Mongols, about the middle of the thirteenth century.

It is interesting to notice how, both in Europe and in Asia, such rude barbarians as the Mongols, who revelled in rapine and bloodshed and marked their progress with monuments of human skulls, were, like other scavengers of civilisation—the Goths, Vandals, and Huns—the means of moving the intellectual waters and of bringing new inspiration into art.

The effect of the Mongol invasion on the civilisation of Western Asia is well summarised by Professor E. G. Browne in his " Literary History of Persia " :

" Infinitely destructive and disastrous as it was to life, learning and civilisation, and especially to the Arab culture, which, as we have already seen, maintained itself with such extraordinary vitality in Persia for six centuries, long after the war of Arab conquest had utterly subsided, the Mongol invasion did, perhaps, contain some quickening elements, and the Mongol character, for all its reckless ferocity, some potentialities of good. One of its few good effects was the extraordinary intermixture of remote peoples, resulting in a refreshing of somewhat stagnant mental reservoirs, which it brought about. In Europe it was a cause, if not the chief cause of the Renaissance, for it thrust the Ottoman Turks out of the obscurity of Khurāsān into the prominence of Constantinople and was thus ultimately re-

sponsible for the destruction of the Byzantine
Empire and the dispersion of the Greeks and their
treasures into Europe. . . . And within Asia it
brought together, first in conflict and then in
consultation, Persians and Arabs with Chinese
and Tibetans, and confronted, on terms of equa-
lity which had not existed for five or six centuries,
the doctors of Islam with Christian monks,
Buddhist Lamas, Mongol *bakhshīs* or medicine
men, and the representatives of other religions
and sects " (pp. 441–2).

It is very important to remember also that from
motives of self-interest, and not from any respect
for art, these ferocious invaders, who massacred
wholesale men, women, and children of the
general population, usually spared the artisans
and craftsmen, and thus preserved for their own
uses the art-traditions of the countries they
ravaged and desolated. Skilled craftsmen were
always the prizes of war, and when an uncivilised
race like the Mongols triumphed over a highly
cultivated one the craftsmen of the defeated
became the teachers of the victors ; this trans-
plantation into a new soil brought new vigour
into art, and was the beginning of great developments. When Timur, the ancestor of the Indian
Mogul dynasty, withdrew his hordes from
northern India in 1398, after ravaging it with
fire and sword, he took back with him as captives
all the masons who had built the famous mosque

14

of Ferozabad, in order that they might build one
like it at Samarkand.   Thus Indian art fulfilled
once more its civilising mission, and when two
and a half centuries later Timur's descendant
Shah Jahān was building the famous Tāj Mahall
at Agra, some of the principal masons were
brought from Samarkand—probably descendants
of Timur's captives.

The important part which craftsmen, more
especially oriental craftsmen, have always played
in the world's history as missionaries of civilisation, culture, and religion, is not generally recognised by bookmen.   Even at the present day the
Indian craftsman, deeply versed in his *Silpā-
śāstras*, learned in folk-lore and in national epic
literature, though excluded from Indian universities—or rather, on that account—is often more
highly cultured intellectually and spiritually than
the average Indian graduate.   In medieval times
the craftsman's intellectual influence, being creative and not merely assimilative, was at least as
great as that of the priest and bookman.   The
Founder of Christianity was Himself a craftsman,
and in those noblest monuments of the Christian
faith—the Gothic cathedrals of medieval Europe
—we can see that the splendid craftsmen of the
Middle Ages preached and practised a religion like
their Master's, pure and undefiled before God,
while philosophers and bookmen wrangled over
its dogmas.

It is curious that archæologists, who are so concerned in trying to prove that nearly all Indian art was derived from the West, should seem to be only dimly aware of the immeasurably greater debt which European art and science owe to India, for they very rarely dwell upon it. From the time of the break-up of the Roman Empire, and even some centuries before, down to the days of the Renaissance, there was flowing into Europe a continuous undercurrent of Indian science, philosophy, and art, brought by the art-workers of the East. In the nature of things, what could have been the effect of Alexander's raid, or even the more lasting influence of the Græco-Baktrian kingdom, compared with that of the successive streams of Asiatic invaders (barbarians, if you will) which century after century poured into Europe, bringing with their armies skilled craftsmen as engineers and armourers, followed by artisans of every kind, when, as often happened, a permanent occupation of a country took place ?

Even uncultured marauders, like the Huns and Mongols, brought with them non-combatant craftsmen to help them in their attacks on walled towns, and to keep their fighting equipment in order ; so that, while the fighting men of East and West were busy cutting throats, the craftsmen of both sides fraternised in a secret freemasonry, founded on common artistic interests.

Indian idealism during the greater part of this time was the dominant note of the art of Asia which was thus brought into Europe ; and when we find a perfectly Oriental atmosphere and strange echoes of Eastern symbolism in the medieval cathedrals of Europe, and see their structural growth gradually blossoming with all the exuberance of Eastern imagery, it is impossible to avoid the conclusion that Gothic architecture and Gothic handicraft owe very much to the absorption, by the *bauhütten* of Germany and other Western craft-guilds, of Asiatic science and art, brought by the thousands of Asiatic craftsmen who entered Europe in the first millennium of the Christian era ; a period which in the minds of Europeans is generally a blank because the " Great Powers " were then located in Asia instead of in Europe.

Byzantine art and Gothic art derived their inspiration from the same source—the impact of Asiatic thought upon the civilisation of the Roman Empire. The first shows its effect upon the art of the Greek and Latin races, the other its influence upon the Romanesque art of the Teutonic and Celtic races. The spirit of Indian idealism breathes in the mosaics of St. Mark's at Venice, just as it shines in the mystic splendours of the Gothic cathedrals ; through the delicate tracery of their jewelled windows, filled with the stories of saints and martyrs ; in all their richly sculptured arches, fairy vaulting, and soaring pinnacles and spires. The Italian Renaissance marks the reversion of Christian art to the pagan ideals of Greece, and the capture of art by the bookmen, leading to our present dilettantism and archæological views of art.

When a new inspiration comes into European art it will come again from the East ; but what irony there is in the present spectacle of the Christian nations of Europe, in the twentieth century, using their influence to paganise the art of Asia !

To return to the history of Mogul art—the revival of painting in Persia under Mogul rule was very largely due to the influence of the Chinese schools, which again owed their inspiration originally to the great schools of India. In the early centuries of the Christian era the traditions of Indian religious art had been brought into Turkestan and China by Indian Buddhist missionaries and craftsmen, and by Chinese students taught in Indian universities. There they were acclimatised, and by the fusion of Indian idealism with the naturalism of the indigenous schools the modern schools of China and Japan originated, which are more familiar to European artists and art critics than the art of India, to which they owe so much.

Under this Indian inspiration Chinese painting had reached by the seventh century (which may be considered as the zenith of pictorial art in India) an extraordinary degree of eminence, far surpassing the contemporary art of Europe. Dr. W. Anderson, in his great work on Japanese and Chinese painting, says :

" There is, perhaps, no section of art that has been so completely misapprehended in Europe as the pictorial art of China. For us the Chinese painter, past or present, is but a copyist who imitates with laborious and indiscriminating exactness whatever is laid before him, rejoices in the display of as many and as brilliant colours as his subject and remuneration will permit, and is only original in the creation of monstrosities.

" Nothing could be more contrary to fact than this impression. If we omit from consideration the work executed for the foreign market—work which every educated Chinese would disown— the old Masters of the Middle Kingdom, who as a body united grandeur of conception with immense power of execution, cared little for elaboration of detail, and except in Buddhist pictures sought their best effects in the simplicity of black and white, or in the most subdued chromatic harmonies. . . .

" If we endeavour to compare the pictorial art of China with that of Europe, we must carry ourselves back to the days when the former was in its greatness. It may be safely asserted that nothing produced by the painters of Europe between the seventh and thirteenth centuries approaches within measurable distance of the works of the great Chinese masters who gave lustre to the T'ang, Sung, and Yuën dynasties ; nor— to draw a little nearer to modern times—is there anything in the religious art of Cimabue that would not appear tame and graceless by the side of the Buddhistic compositions of Wu-Tao-Tsz', Li Lung-yen, and Ngan Huru. Down to the end of the Southern Empire in 1279 A.D., the Chinese were at the head of the world in the art of painting, as in many things besides, and their nearest rivals were their own pupils, the Japanese."[1]

The artists of this new Iranian school of painting, revived by an infusion of Indian art traditions naturalised in China, were the court painters of Bābur, the first Mogul Emperor of India, who thus brought them back to the fountain-head of their art. But Mogul painting was, unlike Indian, a purely secular school. The general ban of the fine arts was not removed even by the Mogul Emperors, and it continued to have full effect so far as religious art was concerned.

Painting as a fine art became a diversion for the Mogul Emperors and their nobles ; the artists of the courts of Akbar, Jahāngīr, and Shah Jahān, both Hindu and Muhammadan, were greatly encouraged, in drawing portraits, in illustrating legend and history or contemporary life, both in fresco on the walls of palaces and villas and in exquisite miniature paintings on paper, usually

[1] " Pictorial Art in Japan," vol. ii, p. 262.

intended for book illustration. But not even
Akbar, who took a most liberal and enlightened
view of art, permitted the representation of a
human being, or of the Deity, in a mosque or
building consecrated to religion. Nor did he
attempt to revive a school of religious painting.
The rule of the Sunna is scrupulously observed in
the decoration of the great mosque at Fatehpur-
Sikri, where Akbar promulgated his new religion,
" The Divine Faith."

The fresco paintings of the Mogul period, like
those of Hindu times, have nearly all perished,
only a few fragments remaining of the decoration
of Akbar's palace at Fatehpur-Sikri.[1]

Our present knowledge of Mogul painting is
almost entirely derived from the pictures, nearly
always painted on very fine Indian or Chinese
paper, which in spite of the delicate material
have more often survived, as they were frequently
carefully preserved in royal libraries or in private
collections.

In early Mogul times oil painting was not
practised by Indian artists, and it should be
understood that these pictures by the Mogul
court painters were not, as a rule, hung on the
walls of apartments, or used for decoration, like
modern European cabinet pictures. The pictures

[1] The most interesting of these is a full-length portrait of a lady,
painted on a panel inside the building known as " Miriam's House,"
probably the residence of Mariam Zāmāni, the mother of Jahāngīr.

of the Indian *chitra-sālas* were always painted
directly on the walls in fresco or tempera, but
the Indo-Muhammadan paintings were kept like
valuable manuscripts, and only brought out
occasionally to be handed round for discussion and
criticism ; just as in Japan to-day the painted
silk scrolls, called *kakemonos*, are displayed one
at a time at a tea-party and afterwards carefully
packed away. The refined artistic sense of the
true Oriental dilettante would be outraged by the
hideous jumble of heterogeneous pictures which
we crowd together in modern exhibitions and use
to " decorate " our houses.

The early Mogul paintings, or those dating
from the first half of the sixteenth century, in the
reigns of Bābur and Humāyūn, are all of the
Persian school, which absorbed many Central
Asian elements. The effect of the Islamic ban
on the fine arts is very strongly marked in all of
them. Muhammadan calligraphists were craftsmen of the highest rank, but when they turned to
picture-painting and were released from the rule
prohibiting the delineation of the human form
they took a long time to shake off the tradition
of centuries which had confined them to the
elaboration of geometric patterns. They showed
little of the genius of the old Buddhist mural
painters for vivid narration, for depicting life,
buoyant, throbbing, exalted, stirred by passionate
spiritual impulses. They had an intense delight

in the beauty of a tree or flower, and an unerring intuitive feeling for decorative fitness, but no interest in humanity as a revelation of life. They continued to regard a human figure or crowd with the eye of a geometrical designer, only as a pattern giving opportunities for delightful colour harmonies and intricate combinations of lines. Somewhat in the manner of the modern cubist, only without self-consciousness and aggressiveness, Indo-Muhammadan calligraphists reduced pictorial art to a geometric formula.

The contact of Persia with China and to a certain extent with Europe gradually helped the Muhammadan calligraphers to bring more life into their pictorial efforts, and about the end of the fifteenth century a famous painter Bihzād, at the court of Sultan Husain of Khurasan, founded a new school distinguished by minute finish and careful observation of nature, especially of animal life. It was from this school that Bābur and Humāyūn, the two first Mogul emperors of India, drew most of their court painters.

Nevertheless the gulf which separated them from the early Indian schools of mural painting was very wide. A comparison of a painting by Shapur of Khurasan, who was probably attached to Humāyūn's court, with the Ajantā and Bagh paintings, will show what a world of difference there was between the outlook of the Muham-

A NAUTCH PARTY AT THE COURT OF MUHAMMAD TUGLAK

(By Shapur of Khurasan)

madan artist-scribe and that of the Buddhist
mural painter. Shapur's picture (Plate LV), now
in the Calcutta Art Gallery, is dated 1534 and
represents a nautch party at the court of Muhammad Tuglak—a somewhat similar scene to that
depicted on the walls of Bagh ten or eleven
centuries earlier. Shapur draws his group dia-
grammatically on a rich gold background with the
neatness and precision of an accomplished scribe,
making delicious colour harmonies with a pale
blue carpet and the orange, green, lilac, and
lemon coloured costumes, but the figures, though
well-spaced for decorative effect, seem like pup-
pets pulled by strings compared with the intensely
alive and human group of Indian minstrels and
dancers at Bagh.

It was not until the time of Akbar and of his
son Jahāngīr that the Mogul court painters of
India began to throw off the stiffness and formality of the old tradition, and to draw fresh
inspiration from the study of nature which the
Muhammadan law, as interpreted by the Caliphs,
had denied them.

The new departure was due partly, perhaps, to
the influence of the Hindu painters employed at
the Mogul court, but we need not assume from
Abul Fazl's admiration for their art that Hindu
painting in the sixteenth century retained the
freshness and vitality of the Ajantā school or
that the renaissance of art under the Mogul

Emperors achieved results at all comparable
with the sculpture and painting of pre-Muhammadan times. Judging from the works of
Akbar's Hindu painters which have come down
to us, it would seem that Indian painting, like
Indian poetry, had become intensely formal and
ritualistic. The Hindus were generally more
proficient in drawing the human figure, but both
Hindu and Muhammadan artists seemed to be
cramped by the Islamic tradition, thinking
more of the geometric pattern of the picture,
as providing the framework for their brilliant
colour-schemes, than of the representation of
animate things.

Abul Fazl, Akbar's Prime Minister and devout
admirer, records in the courtly language of the
Aīn-i-Akbāri the Emperor's practical interest in
the fine arts and the prejudices of the orthodox
Musalman :

" I have to notice that the observing of the
figures of objects and the making of likenesses of
them are, for a well-regulated mind, a source of
wisdom, and an antidote against the poison of
ignorance. Bigoted followers of the letter of the
law are hostile to the art of painting, but their
eyes now see the truth.

" One day, at a private party of friends, His
Majesty, who had conferred on several the pleasure of drawing near him, remarked : ' There are
many that hate painting, but such men I

dislike. It appears to me as if a painter had quite peculiar means of recognising God, for a painter, in sketching anything that has life, and in devising the limbs one after another, must come to feel that he cannot bestow personality upon his work, and is thus forced to thank God the Giver of Life, and will thus increase his knowledge.'

"Akbar," says Abul Fazl, "had from his earliest youth shown a great interest in painting, and given it every encouragement, regarding it both as a means of study and as an amusement.

"The works of all painters are weekly laid before His Majesty by the Darogahs and the clerks; he then confers rewards according to excellence of workmanship, or increases the monthly salaries. Much progress was made in commodities required by painters, and the correct prices of such articles carefully ascertained. The mixture of colour has especially been improved. The pictures thus received a hitherto unknown finish.

"Most excellent painters are now to be found and masterpieces worthy of a Bihzād may be placed at the side of the wonderful works of the European painters who have attained world-wide fame. The minuteness in detail, the general finish, the boldness of execution, etc., now observed in pictures are incomparable; even inanimate objects look as if they had life. More than a hundred painters have become famous masters of the art, while the number of those who approach perfection, or those who are middling, is very large. This is especially true of the

Hindus : their pictures surpass our conception of things. Few indeed in the whole world are found equal to them.

"The number of masterpieces of painting increased with the encouragement given to the art. Persian books, both prose and poetry, were ornamented with pictures, and a very large number of paintings were thus collected. The story of Hamzah was represented in twelve volumes, and clever painters made the most astonishing illustrations for no less than one thousand and four hundred passages of the story. The 'Chingiz-namah,' the 'Zafar-nameh,' this book, the 'Razm-nameh,' the 'Ramayan,' the 'Nal Daman,' the 'Kalilah Damnah,' the 'Ayār Dāmsh,' etc., were all illustrated.

"His Majesty himself sat for his likeness,[1] and also ordered to have the likenesses taken of all the grandees of the realm. An immense album was thus formed ; those that have passed away have received a new life, and those that are still alive have immortality promised them."[2]

Abul Fazl gives a list of the celebrated painters of the Court. He singles out four for special mention :

"Mir Sayyid Ali, of Tabriz." [Translator's note : "Better known as a poet, under the name of Juddi. He illuminated the story of Amir Hamzah, mentioned above."]

---

[1] A portrait of Akbar, bearing Jahāngīr's seal, formerly in the Calcutta Art Gallery, is now in the Victoria Memorial Collection.

[2] Blochmann's translation, vol. i, pp. 107 et seq.

" Kwājah Abduççamad, styled Shīrīnqalam, or ' Sweet Pen.' He comes from Shiraz.

" Daswanth. He is the son of a palkee-bearer. He devoted his whole life to the art, and used, from love to his profession, to draw and paint figures even on walls. One day the eye of His Majesty fell on him ; his talent was discovered, and he himself handed over to the Kwājah. In a short time he surpassed all painters and became the first master of the age. Unfortunately the light of his talents was dimmed by the shadow of madness. He committed suicide. He has left many masterpieces.

" Basāwan. In backgrounding, drawing of features, distribution of colours, portrait-painting, and several other branches, he is most excellent. So much so that many critics prefer him to Daswanth."

The following thirteen painters are also mentioned as being famous :

Kesu, Zāl, Mukund, Mushkin, Farrukh the Qalmaq, Mādhū, Jagan, Mohesh, K'hemkaran, Tārā, Sānwlah, Haribans, Rām.

A considerable number of the works of these painters are still in existence, and in the last twenty years have emerged from obscurity and furnished materials for many learned critical studies which have done much to create an interest in Indian art, at least as a cult for the connoisseur, if not in a deeper sense. It is impossible here to enter into all the technical details which are of such absorbing interest for the collector.

Akbar was certainly something more than a connoisseur. He approached art in a religious spirit and with a profound view of statesmanship, regarding it as a spiritual force which makes for peace, reconciliation, and enlightenment. The early works of his court painters, such as the illustrations of the story of Amir Hamzah and of the Akbar-nāma, exhibit a patchwork of all the contemporary calligraphic styles, Persian, Central Asian, Chinese, and Indian, the predominant tendency being towards fine pattern-making, more suggestive of Chinese cloisonné enamel and faience than of pictorial art, as it is understood in Europe. Akbar's aim apparently was to create a new synthesis of art out of all the heterogeneous racial elements which were gathered in his court in the same way as he sought to unite all the religious elements in his imperial Order, the Dīn-i-Ilāhi; his method being to bring out individual talent by the spur of competition under his own eye. Eventually a definite Mogul style which was really Indian evolved out of this clash of racial æsthetics, but, as Dr. Heinrich Gluck remarks in his sumptuous volume on the Hamzah series in the Vienna Museum of Art and Industry, painting under Akbar and his successors

" became a thing which was specially perfected

in certain departments, e.g. portraiture and group-portraiture, but which invariably remained confined to the court and to which somehow the character of the conscious and of something artificially produced ever clings. For it is true that at a later period this art also came, here and there, into touch with popular sources, but very much as an eccentric wealthy man surrounds himself with a collection of popular objects. This art was not produced out of the unconscious popular spirit, out of the crystallisation of this spirit in a dominant will, and therefore could not flow back into it." [1]

Yet it must be remembered that Akbar's personal influence extended over almost the whole range of art and must not be reckoned solely by the works of his court painters. He was a great builder, and the numerous state-workshops which he established and supervised with his indefatigable energy were admirable schools of arts and crafts. But Akbar's reign was a period of transition and reconstruction, and his influence upon the art of his time was most apparent after his death.

Jahāngīr, Akbar's intemperate son (1605–28), inherited few of his father's higher qualities, but was equally devoted to the fine arts. His memoirs contain many evidences of the keen personal, even affectionate, interest which he took in his court painters and their work. He treated

[1] Translated in " Rūpam," No. 29, Jan. 1927.

15

them as intimate friends and frequently bestowed upon them the highest distinctions. Jahāngīr himself tells us that he raised Sherif Khan, the son of Abdul Hamad—one of Akbar's portrait-painters—who had grown up with him from infancy and upon whom, while heir-apparent, he had conferred the title of Khan, to the position of premier grandee of the empire.

In the thirteenth year of his reign the memoirs record :

" This day Abul Hasan, a painter who bore the name of Nādiru-Zamān, drew a picture of my court and presented it to me. He had attached it as a frontispiece to the 'Jahāngīr-nāma.' As it was well worthy of praise, I loaded him with great favours. If the celebrated Abul Haī and Bihzād were alive they would do him full justice for his exalted taste in painting.

" His father, Aka-Rāza, was always with me when I was a prince and his son was born in my household. However, the son is far superior to his father. I gave him a good education, till he became one of the most distinguished men of the age. The portraits furnished by him are beautiful.

" Mansūr is also a master of the art of drawing and he has the title of Nādiru-l-Aslī. In the time of my father and my own there have been none to compare with these two artists."

Neither Abul Hasan nor Mansūr is mentioned in Abul Fazl's list. They came into prominence in the later period of Akbar's reign. Mansūr is chiefly known for his wonderful studies of bird life, which are noticed further on, but he was also one of the best of the Mogul portrait-painters.

Jahāngīr prides himself on his ability as a connoisseur and alludes to the practice of dividing the work of painting a picture between several artists :

" I am very fond of pictures, and have such a discrimination in judging them that I can tell the name of the artist, whether living or dead. If there are several portraits (in the same picture) painted by several artists I could point out the painter of each. Even if one portrait were finished by several painters I could mention the names of those who had drawn the different portions of that single picture. In fact I could declare without fail by whom the brow and by whom the eyelashes were drawn, or if anyone had touched up the portrait after it was drawn by the first painter."

When his zoological collection was enriched by a number of rare birds and animals from Goa he ordered paintings to be made from them, and observes :

" The Emperor Bābur has in his memoirs given an able description and pictured representation of several animals ; but it is most probable that he never ordered the painters to draw them from the life."

It was, no doubt, the practice of drawing from the living model, enjoined by Akbar and Jahāngīr on their painter-calligraphists, which led to the very remarkable achievements in portraiture and direct representation of animal life of the best artists of Jahāngīr and Shah Jahān. This practice and the division of labour in making up a picture to which Jahāngīr alludes may also account for the disjointed design of many of the Mogul paintings. The miniature painters of the Mogul School painted as exquisitely as the *petits maîtres* of Europe, but they cannot be put in the same class as the great masters of Ajantā and Bagh, who followed their own traditions and were not under dilettante dictation. The painters of the Hindu School, whose superiority as artists impressed Abul Fazl so strongly, did not take " drawing from the life " in the same sense as the modern European academician. It did not mean that the student sat down in front of his model and reproduced as closely as possible the reflection of it on the retina of his own eyes ; but that after the most careful observation he went away to record his mental impression of it, returning occasionally, if necessary, to refresh his memory. In this way the artist's memory and powers of observation were developed to an extraordinary degree, as we can see in the wonderful memory paintings of the Ajantā and Bagh viharas.

An amusing passage in the memoirs of Sir

Thomas Roe, who was sent by James I to the
Court of the Great Mogul in the interests of the
East India Company, is concerned with Jahāngīr's pride in the technical skill of his painters.
The directors of the Company knowing what
were the most acceptable presents at the Mogul
Court had sent some pictures with the ambassador:
they had previously sent out portraits of James
and his Queen, Anne of Denmark, as well as
one of Sir Thomas Smyth, Governor of the Company, which was much prized by Jahāngīr as his
painters, so it was said, confessed their inability
to imitate it.

Finding that Jahāngīr was more pleased with
pictures than with anything else, Roe presented
him with one of his own :

" A Pickture of a friend of myne that I esteemed
very much, and was for Curiositye rare, which I
would give his Maiestie as a present, seeing hee so
much affected that art ; assuring myselfe he
never saw any equall to it, neyther was anything
more esteemed of mee."

This was a painting by Isaac Oliver, the English
miniaturist.

Jahāngīr was delighted with the picture, but
offered to bet with the ambassador that his own
painters would make a copy of it which Roe
could not distinguish from the original. After
some diplomatic fencing, Roe, who had formed a

very poor opinion of Indian artists, agreed to
" lay a good horse " with the Minister, Asaph
Khan ; but the latter, he noted in his diary,
" recanted in Priuat."

Some weeks afterwards the ambassador was
summoned to the Durbar and was first asked by
Jahāngīr what he would give the painter if his
copy fulfilled the terms of the wager.

" A painter's reward—50 rupees," said Sir
Thomas, rather contemptuously. Jahāngīr replied that this was insufficient, for his painter
was " a Cauallero "—a gentleman. The copies,
when produced, were five in number, pasted
together with the original " on one table," and
so like that Roe was—

" By candlelight troubled to discerne which was
which ; I confess beyond all expectation ; yet I
showed myne owne and the differences which
were in arte apparent, but not to be judged by a
common eye. But for that at first sight I knew
it not, hee [Jahāngīr] was very merry and joyfull,
and craked like a Northern man."

Jahāngīr again exultingly insisted upon knowing what reward Roe would give to his painter,
and refusing a gift of money, finally settled that
for one of the copies which Jahāngīr gave, the
artist should choose one of the English " toyes"
Roe had brought with him.

Though the test imposed by Jahāngīr was one

of ordinary technical skill and not very convincing, there is no doubt that there were many
distinguished artists among his court painters.
The subtle refinement of the Indian miniaturist's
art was evidently lost upon Roe, and the more
obvious realism of European painting appealed
to him, just as it does to " a common eye " in
India to-day.

It is interesting to note that about this time
one of the greatest of European artists, Rembrandt, was making use of Indian miniature
paintings in his work. Among Rembrandt's pen-
and-ink studies collected in the British Museum
a number have been identified as copies or adapta-
tions of Indian miniatures, and it has been shown
that from them chiefly Rembrandt derived the
atmosphere for his Biblical subjects.

Professor Sarre, in his monograph on the subject,[1] compares reproductions of the original
Mogul miniatures with Rembrandt's pen-and-ink
sketches. The British Museum possesses a drawing by Rembrandt copied from a Mogul miniature
of " Akbar (?) [2] on his Throne," now in the Ethnographic Museum, Berlin. The latter has also an
original Mogul painting of an " Indian Prince on
Horseback," of which Rembrandt's copy is in
the British Museum. The Louvre has another

[1] " Jahrbuch den Kön. Preuszischen Kunst Sammlungen,"
xxv, Berlin, 1904.
[2] Mr. G. P. Rouffaer has pointed out that this is Jahāngīr.

study by him of " Timur on his Throne," copied, with a few variations, from an Indian miniature now in Berlin.

It appears that in 1631 Rembrandt resided at Amsterdam, then the headquarters of the Dutch East India Company. In 1642 he painted the portrait of Abraham Wilmerdonks, a Director of the Company, who had a considerable oriental collection.

Rembrandt himself collected oriental costumes, wood-carving, and paintings. In the inventory of his effects made after his bankruptcy in 1656, there is an entry of " a book of curious miniature drawings," which may have been the Mogul miniatures from which he made his studies.

Professor Sarre is doubtless right in pointing out that, though Rembrandt made use of these miniatures for the oriental accessories of his pictures, it cannot be said that his art was influenced by them in a deeper sense. European critics do not always show such discernment when they discover Indian artists borrowing Western details for their own use.

Both Akbar and Jahāngīr admired the realism of the European paintings which were brought to them as presents. They had them copied and hung them on the walls of their palaces as modern Indian Princes do. The best Mogul painters used them in their original work in the same way as Rembrandt and many Italian masters used

PLATE LVI

TWO BRUSH-LINE PORTRAITS, SCHOOL OF SHAH JAHĀN

oriental material, not imitatively but artistically. Indian art thus preserved the intrinsic qualities which give it value and interest to Western artists. When it loses its Indianness it loses everything.

The middle of Shah Jahān's reign (1628–58) may be said to mark the zenith of the Mogul Court painters' art, though there is no record of such intimate personal relations between the Emperor and his artists as that which Jahāngīr has given us. The unhappy Dārā Shikoh, Shah Jahān's eldest son, has left a token of his personal interest in painting in the album which is now one of the historic treasures of the India Office Library. It is dedicated to his cousin and favourite wife, " his nearest and dearest friend, the Lady Nādirah Begum," in the year 1051 A.H. (A.D. 1641–2). Her tragic fate, seventeen years later, is told by Tavernier. She died of heat and thirst in the deserts of Sind, while following her husband in his flight from the victorious forces of Aurangzīb. Dārā Shikoh himself, distraught with grief, was betrayed into his brother's hands shortly afterwards and murdered in prison.

The sorrowful story lends a pathetic interest to the fine portrait of the Prince as a youth gazing at his beloved's picture (Plate LIX), now in the Victoria Memorial Collection, Calcutta, which will be noticed later on.

The accession of Aurangzīb in 1658 completely

altered the privileged position which artists had enjoyed at the Mogul Court, and from that time interest is mainly concentrated on the independent Hindu schools, the most important of which were located in Rajputana and Gujarat, and later on in some of the sub-Himalayan principalities.

CHAPTER III

TYPICAL INDIAN MINIATURE PAINTINGS

THERE were, as Abul Fazl indicates, two forma-
tive elements in the school of painting established
by Akbar, one which was mainly foreign, derived
from the different Islamic schools of book-illustra-
tion and calligraphy, the other indigenous and
Hindu, which must also be taken as a general
term for Indian art, derived from folk-traditions
and from the ancient schools of mural painting.
In course of time the two amalgamated and
formed a distinct school, called Mogul to distinguish it both from the foreign schools and from
the contemporary Hindu and Jain schools which
had an independent existence.

The nucleus of the school was formed by the
foreigners brought into India by Bābur and
Humāyūn, but under Akbar the Hindu element
became the strongest both in numbers and as a
creative force, for the Indian painters had an
age-long tradition of art-practice behind them
closely bound up with religious and social life and
only fettered by puritanical restrictions when

they were obliged to consider the feelings of their Muslim rulers. Yet the indigenous schools must have suffered much from the disrepute in which pictorial art was held by Muhammadan orthodoxy and by the strict enforcement of the law of Islam in the previous centuries. A Hindu who wished to avoid offence to his Musalman neighbours, or to cultivate their friendship, would not care to decorate the walls of his guest-chamber with paintings banned by the law of Islam. But he could indulge his personal taste and that of his Hindu friends secretly with the art of the miniature painter.

Abul Fazl only makes a passing allusion to wall-painting. Like every strict Muhammadan he valued calligraphy as a finer art than that of the picture-painter and not suspect as irreligious. " The letter, a magical power, is spiritual geometry, emanating from the pen of invention ; a heavenly writ from the hand of fate." There were eight calligraphical systems recognised in the Muhammadan world. In China writing and drawing have been recognised as sister arts from the days of the legendary monarch Fa-hi in the third millennium B.C. who is said to have made drawing one of the six branches of calligraphy.

The character of the handwriting to which he was accustomed naturally influenced greatly the style of the artist's drawing. The great variety of the strokes in Chinese and Japanese ideographs has given an immense fluency and variety to the brush-outlines of the artists of those countries : in Japan ten different styles of line-drawing are recognised, each style representing a special character or mode of expression. The Indo-Persian scribe, on the other hand, used a reed-pen in writing and as a miniature painter his line acquired thereby more uniformity and regularity, the precision of a medallist rather than the fluency of the habitual brush-writer. Owing to the generally small scale of the Mogul drawings it was a line of wonderful delicacy, though the rhythmic flow of the Ajantā brush-lines, controlled by the arm and wrist rather than by the fingers, is generally wanting. The Ajantā technique is more apparent in the drawings of Hindu artists, who practised both fresco and miniature painting and did not specialise in calligraphy. As they had the predominating influence at the Mogul Court the stiffness and conventionality of the early school of Akbar gradually disappears, though the calligraphic style left its mark on the character of most Mogul painting.

Indian connoisseurs distinguish the various styles of draughtsmanship which developed in different localities or different families of painters by the term *kalam*, pen or brush—the lines being drawn with a fine brush usually made from the hairs of a squirrel's tail.

A preliminary outline sketch was made in

Indian red, used without gum so that when dry
the colour could be brushed away, leaving a very
faint indication of the drawing. The finished
line was then drawn with lamp-black, specially
prepared by burning a camphorated cotton wick
in a mustard-oil lamp. Sometimes the drawing
was delicately shaded, and some of the details
heightened with gold or tinted. The artists
prided themselves on the fineness of their brushes,
and the test of supreme skill was to finish the
detail with an *ek bāl kalam*, a one-haired brush,
which seems to have been used for microscopic
stippling as well as for the finest lines.

The illustrations will give some idea of the great
distinction, delicacy, and charm of the best
Mogul court painters' brush-drawing. With all
the sincerity, truthfulness, and perfect finish of
the old Dutch and Flemish masters, these Indian
drawings have a subtlety and sensitiveness of
their own suggestive of the songs of Hafiz and
Omar Khayyam and of the music of the *vīna* to
which the dilettante of the Mogul Court listened
as the portraits passed from hand to hand. Sometimes delicately shaded and embellished with
discreet touches of gold, they are completely
satisfying as works of art, the strength and sure-
ness of the brush-lines giving them then the precision of fine sculpture.

Plate LVI shows two admirable brush-line
studies by an unknown artist of two of Shah

PLATE LVII

PRINCE MUHAMMAD MURAD ON THE ELEPHANT IQBAL

(From a drawing by Ghulām)

Jahān's courtiers, Mirza Sultan Nazir (left) and Afzal Khan, from Lady Scott-Moncrieff's collection. A more highly finished drawing shaded and embellished with gold, reproduced in Plate LVII, bears the inscription in Persian, " Prince Murad, son of Shah Jahān, on the elephant Iqbal, drawn by Ghulām, 1030 A.H. (A.D. 1621)." Interest is concentrated on the great elephant, which has evidently become unruly, as he is flourishing the mahout's goad in his trunk and trumpeting with rage. The Prince has climbed on his back to take the mahout's place while the latter, or one of the attendants, is chaining the elephant's legs. The excited action of the great beast is splendidly given, while the vigour of the composition is not less striking than the finished technique, both in the drawing of the three elephants and in the careful study of the banyan-tree behind.

In the portrait of Shah Jahān's Poet Laureate, Muhammad Jam Qudsi (Plate LVIII), the artist Bichitr reveals himself as one of the most accomplished masters of the Mogul Court. This delightful coloured drawing, one of the collection made by the author for the Calcutta Art Gallery, bore on the mount an inscription by the court scribe or a former owner, " A Portrait of Sa'di of Shiraz (may God sanctify his tomb !)," but a more authentic inscription on a similar portrait published by Major D. Macaulay in the " Burlington Magazine "[1] gives both the name of the artist and the subject of the portrait as above.

Though it is unmistakably a study from life, it is not surprising that it should be taken for a portrait of the more famous Persian poet of the fourteenth century. There was a regular demand at the Mogul Court for traditional portraits, such as those of the Padshah's ancestors, or other great historical personages, and such portrait types, more or less authentic, were handed down in the artist's families from one generation to another as part of their stock-in-trade.

The dignified old poet of Shah Jahān's Court, with a face so strong and full of character, might very well have posed for the adventurous Sa'di, whose sonnets often served as decoration on the illuminated mounts which framed the Mogul miniatures so exquisitely. When the great masters of calligraphy thus collaborated with the miniature painters the taste of the Mogul connoisseur who gave the frame a higher value than the picture is sometimes hardly to be criticised. The mounts of Jahāngīr's miniatures are often embellished with admirably designed floral patterns, in which may be seen the original suggestions for the *pietra-dura* decoration of the Tāj, wrongly attributed by Anglo-Indian tradition to the French adventurer at Shah Jahān's Court, Austin de Bordeaux.

[1] February, 1925.

PLATE LVIII

MUHAMMAD JĀM QUDSI
SHAH JAHĀN'S POET LAUREATE

PLATE LVIII

MUHAMMAD JAM QUDSI
SHAH JAHĀN'S POET LAUREATE

Calligraphy, however, must be treated as outside the scope of this book, except as an influence
bearing on the art of the Mogul miniature painter.
In Bichitr's drawing, moreover, the artist has
the field to himself, for the mount is a simple one,
discreetly splashed with gold. The strength and
thoroughness of his draughtsmanship can only
be appreciated by examining the original with
a magnifying glass.

Portraiture and brilliant court ceremonials were
the subjects of most of the Mogul miniature
paintings. The Padshah and his favourite
generals and courtiers were drawn and painted,
singly and in groups, assembled in Durbar, in
shooting or hawking parties, sometimes in battles
or sieges. The illustrations to the Akbar-nāma
give vivid impressions of the great Emperor's
manifold activities, but are more interesting as
historical documents than as works of art. A
rigid code of etiquette prevents the artist from
penetrating deeply the human side of Mogul
Court life. Religious subjects are studiously
avoided, except for a formal visit to a sacred
shrine, or an interview with a Muslim saint.

Restricted to a very limited range of ceremonial
poses, nearly always in profile, the court portrait-
painters could yet show their high capacity as
delineators of character, while they revelled in
delicate finish and in gem-like combinations of
colour, which gave currency to the legend that
16

they used precious stones as pigments. The best
Mogul miniatures, therefore, have a high æsthetic
value, apart from their historical importance,
in spite of the artificial atmosphere in which the
artists lived.

The portrait (*Frontispiece*) of Sultan Muhammad Kutb Shah of Golconda, by Mir Hashim,
one of Shah Jahān's court painters, might be
taken to represent the acme of elegance and
distinction attained in Mogul painted portraiture.
In the fine sensitive drawing of the head and
hands Mir Hashim shows himself Bichitr's equal.
Like the latter he has got entirely free from the
somewhat tiresome mannerisms of the calligraphic school, while retaining its cameo-like
precision and delicacy of finish. The conventional
profile pose is made natural and unaffected, the
perpendicular lines of the long sword and the
fall of the brocaded edges of the Sultan's muslin
shawl giving it a statuesque dignity. The pearly
hues of the white drapery, faultlessly rendered,
are set off by sparkling contrasts of emerald, ruby,
gold, and jade. Other Mogul portraits may show
a more sumptuous palette and subtler gradations
of colour, but few have the brilliancy and charm
of this little gem of Mogul art. It seems to
suggest a wall painting in miniature, and as
mural decoration, life-size, it would have been a
noble ornament for the Sultan's palace.

Jahāngīr was as fond of decorating the walls

PLATE LIX

PRINCE DĀRĀ SHIKOH

of his summer-palaces with pictures, especially portraits, as the old Hindu rulers had been. We occasionally get direct evidence of the art of the *chitra-sāla* in Mogul times in large-scale portraits drawn or painted on paper. An exceptionally fine example is the painting reproduced in Plate LIX, which gives a very sympathetic presentment of Dārā Shikoh as a youth, by an unknown artist. The Prince is painted quarter-length, standing within one of the white marble balconies of the Delhi Palace, holding in his hand a portrait of " his nearest and dearest friend," the Lady Nādirah Begum. Rich colour contrasts are obtained by an effective use of silken purdahs and awnings, but the *pietra-dura* decoration of the architectural setting is rather weak and over-elaborated. The portrait itself, drawn with great sincerity and feeling, and delicately modelled in the manner of the later Ajantā School, gives us an insight into the temperament of the high-minded but headstrong Prince. The melancholy mood of a lover or a foreboding of the tragic end of the devoted couple is reflected on his refined but rather effeminate features.

A remarkable but less sympathetic portrait of Dārā Shikoh in later life, on a still larger scale, is given by Mr. Percy Brown in his " Indian Paintings under the Mughals," Plate XXIX. It is by Hunhar, a very able Hindu artist, *c.* 1650.

Ustād Mansūr, upon whom Jahāngīr bestowed

the title of " Wonder of the Age," was one of the
most famous of the Mogul portrait-painters,
though comparison of his known works with
those of Bichitr and Mir Hashim is hardly to his
advantage. The Wantage Collection at the Victoria and Albert Museum has a portrait by him of
Khwāja Kalān Beg which gives the impression of
being an excellent likeness of an obsequious old
courtier, bordering on senile decay, but it lacks
the freshness of Bichitr's and Mir Hashim's
technique, and the elaborate stippling of the
drapery, in imitation perhaps of European miniatures, is rather overdone.

Mansūr's claim to distinction rests rather upon
his admirable portraiture of birds and animals.
The atmosphere of the court under Jahāngīr and
Shah Jahān was too materialistic to produce
devout lovers of nature like the Chinese and
Japanese, or the Indian Buddhist painters. Mansūr, Manohar, and others were only permitted to
study birds and animals as zoological ornaments
of the Mogul Court, posing for their portraits as
the Padshah's protégés, never whirling in flight
across the heavens or enjoying the freedom of
the forest.

Not that Jahāngīr himself did not feel delight
in the beauties of nature : his memoirs give
sufficient proof of his keen artistic temperament.
But he lacked the sincere religious feeling of his
father, and was too self-centred to inspire great

PLATE LX

A TURKEY-COCK

(By Ustād Mansūr)

art. Yet within the limitations imposed by the environment in which they were produced the studies of bird and animal life by Mansūr and Manohar are unsurpassed for scientific exactness and superb craftsmanship.

Jahāngīr mentions the occasion which led him to give orders for a series of paintings from his zoological collection to adorn the pages of the Jahāngīrī-nāma. Mukarrah Khan in the seventh year of his reign had been sent on a mission to Goa, and returned with some rare birds and animals which Jahāngīr had never seen before. Among them was a turkey-cock, of which Jahāngīr gives a graphic description :

" One of the birds resembled a peahen, but was a little larger in size, though less than a peacock. When he was desirous of pairing he used to spread his tail and feathers and danced about like a peacock. His beak and feet resembled those of a barn-door fowl. His head, neck, and throat changed their colour every minute, and when anxious to pair he became a perfect red and seemed to be a beautiful piece of coral. After some time he was as white as cotton, and sometimes he got as blue as a turquoise, and in short turned all colours, like a chameleon. The piece of flesh which is attached to his head looks like the comb of a cock. But the curious part of it was that that piece of flesh, when he was about to pair, hung down a span long, like the trunk of an elephant, and when again restored to its position it was erected over the head to the height of two fingers. The part round his eyes remained constantly of a blue colour, and was never subject to change, which was not the case with his wings, which were always changing their colour, contrary to those of a peacock." [1]

This turkey-cock is the subject of one of Mansūr's best studies (Plate LX), now in the collection of the Calcutta Art Gallery. It bears the imperial seal and is mounted on a magnificent specimen of calligraphy, embellished with flowers of the Kashmir valley, the beauty of which attracted Jahāngīr so much that he employed Mansūr in painting a series of them. The Wantage Collection of the Victoria and Albert Museum has another painting of the turkey and several other fine bird-studies by Mansūr, including the admirable painting of two Indian *sāras* (Plate LXI), probably the portraits of the two pet birds to which Jahāngīr gave the name of Majnūn and Lailā. This is the nearest approach to romance in real life which Jahāngīr's portrait-painters give us. The Padshah's own romance, his attachment to Nūr Jahān, was not a subject for the painter's brush. None of the so-called portraits of her can be considered authentic.

Among other pet animals portrayed by Jahāngīr's artists was a black buck, used as a decoy in hunting. Two very fine studies of it by Manohar

[1] Translated by Elliott, " History of India," vol. vi, pp. 331-2.

PLATE LXI

TWO SĀRAS
By Ustād Mansūr)

are known, one of which (Plate LXII) is in the British Museum and the other in the Wantage Collection at South Kensington.

The Mogul painters naturally took infinite pains in depicting the glitter and tinsel of court ceremonial with all its sumptuous paraphernalia—brocaded canopies and silken carpets, costly jewellery and golden thrones—as a great number of gorgeously decorative paintings testify. But the exuberant elaboration of works of this class, more calligraphic than pictorial, loses all its finesse and colour-charm in reproduction. The subtler qualities of Mogul art are more conspicuous in individual portraiture and in genre painting.

Bichitr shows his quality as a genre painter in his picture (Plate LXIII) called " The Tambura Player," for want of a more explanatory title, in the Wantage Collection at South Kensington. It is a very piquant little scene, closely studied from life, in which a one-eyed musician is singing with great gusto a song which excites the hilarity of his listener, the bowman holding an arrow in his left hand and apparently beating time with his right foot. The facial expression of both is admirably rendered, and the imperturbable countenance of the servant squatting in the foreground, with his bundle between his legs, is equally true to life.

The realism of this remarkable little picture

might suggest that Bichitr was trying to imitate European painters of genre, but more likely it only points to the natural bent of Mogul art when it shook off the traditional conventions of the calligraphic school. The Mogul Court painters were temperamentally realists, and therefore inclined to admire the realism of the European pictures they saw. But, except under Jahāngīr's dictation, they did not copy them as the modern Indian student does, consciously or unconsciously at the suggestion of his European teachers. They saw life as a materialist sees it, not as a poet or mystic, but did not borrow European spectacles to see it with. They had not the spiritual vision of the Ajantā School, but they were quite sincere students of nature and had someting interesting to say about it. Within their limited range the Indian painters of the Mogul Court kept alive the great traditions of the Ajantā School.

But to appreciate the qualities in Hindu painting which are intimately related to Indian life and thought one must get away from the rather stuffy atmosphere of the Mogul Court into the fresher air of the provinces of the empire, where art had always grown freely under natural conditions, not merely as an exotic cultivated by pampered æsthetes who rebelled against puritanical laws. Here, both in subject-matter and in æsthetic quality, we come at once into contact with the romance of Indian life which was hardly

PLATE LXII

A BLACK BUCK

(By Manohar)

ever touched by the artists of the Delhi Court :
themes of the country-side, its myths and legends,
passionate stories of court-life told by the village
kathak, even glimpses of life behind the zanana
walls.

India has never had any separate school of
landscape painting, like China and Japan, but
in landscape settings to figure subjects of this
kind Hindu painters of the Mogul period and
later, show a full appreciation of the true function
of fine art, as Emerson has nobly expressed it in
his Essay :

" In landscapes the painter should give the
suggestion of a fairer creation than we know.
The details, the prose of Nature, he should omit,
and give us only the spirit and the splendour.
He should know that the landscape has beauty to
the eye because it expresses the thought which is
to him good, and this because the same power
which sees through his eyes is seen in that spectacle ; and he will come to value the expression
of Nature, and not Nature itself, and so exalt
in his copy the features which please him. He
will give the gloom of gloom and the sunshine of
sunshine."

Night and effects of artificial light have an
especial attraction for the Indian painter of
Mogul times, though in his thoughts of night
there is seldom a connotation of fear. It is
rather as the joyful time when lovers meet, or as

the day's nirvāna, when the pure white lotus of heavenly bliss is open, a time for meditation and spiritual gladness, that he feels it.

Plate LXIV, probably a late eighteenth-century work, illustrates the romantic story of Bāz Bahādur, the Mogul governor of Mālwā, and his love for the beautiful Rajput poetess, Rūp Mati. They are seen riding by night through the wooded hills of Mandu, an attendant walking on foot between them; a masalchi in front shows the way with a lighted torch. The darkness closes round the group and pursues the torch's glare. Rūp Mati is pointing eagerly forward; the crescent moon peeps behind a hill and there is a glimpse of a river in the plain below. The blaze of the torch throws the high-mettled steeds and their riders into a warm relief of vivid colour between the darkness and the light, half-revealing, half-obscuring the precipitous rocks behind fringed by a strip of forest. Through the gap between the hills the sky is seen faintly lighted by the moon.

The largeness and simplicity of the treatment are qualities which modern European painters of the impressionist school have often aimed at, but seldom realised with so much spontaneity and true poetry as this little Indian picture, for here there is no conscious effort to produce an effect called artistic, but unaffected interpretation of Nature as it revealed itself to the artist.

PLATE LXIII

THE TAMBURA PLAYER

By Bichitr

Compared with the more sophisticated works of the Mogul Court painters the drawing of the figures and horses is naïve and primitive, though the design shows a fine sense of dignity and rhythmic beauty. Any lack of academic learning is more than atoned for by its romantic charm.

The orthodox critic in Europe is inclined to treat impressionism as a somewhat peculiar development in modern art, towards which he ought to maintain a strictly guarded, if not hostile attitude. It is sometimes a speciality, but more often a fad. To the academic professor it is a dangerous tendency, almost a vice, which should be sternly repressed in all students. The true oriental artist regards it as the breath of life, the end of all art ; he thinks that of all artistic faculties, the one which must be trained and developed to the highest degree is the faculty of realising thought-impressions.

But his impressionism is not merely a blurred vision of natural appearances, as it often is in modern European art. To see with the mind, not merely with the eye ; to bring out the essential quality, not the common appearance of things ; to give the movement and character in a figure, not only the bone and muscle ; to reveal some precious quality or effect in a landscape, not merely physiographical or botanical facts ; and, above all, to identify himself with the inner consciousness of the Nature he portrays, and to make manifest the one harmonious law which governs Nature in all her moods,—these are the thoughts which he always keeps uppermost in his mind as soon as he knows how to use his tools with tolerable facility. It is considered of the most vital importance to train the faculty of mind-seeing from the earliest youth, when impressions are strong and vivid, instead of leaving this development to the end of his academic career, as we usually do in Europe. The oriental artist does not neglect detail—witness the wonderful studies of Japanese masters, and those by Indian artists here illustrated. But the first principle of oriental art-practice is to develop a habit of concentrated thought at the same time as imitative skill is being acquired by practice. In modern European academies the creative power usually lies dormant in the most important years of a student's mental development, while the imitative skill is accumulated by a dreary routine of more or less mechanical exercises. In this respect art teaching only repeats the errors of what we miscall "classical education" in public schools; but the habit thereby engendered of regarding art as a technical process, rather than a creative faculty, explains to a great extent the archæological critic's standpoint in regard to Indian art.

"Deer-hunting by Night," Plate LXV, is another characteristic example in which the artist is more engrossed with the beauty of the

PLATE LXIV

BĀZ BAHĀDUR AND RŪP MATI

night than with the action of the figures. It probably illustrates the story of Rāma and Sītā's exile in the forest by the banks of the Godāvari. The hunters are scantily dressed like forest hermits. The woman, concealed behind a bush, holds a lantern and tinkles a small bell to attract the herd of deer. The man armed with bow and arrows has just shot the leader of the herd, the terrified does scattering in all directions. The gleam of the lantern is given by discreet touches of gold.

The interest of the picture does not, however, lie in the figures, but in the charm of the landscape setting and serenity of its translucent chiaroscuro, which makes one feel the stillness of the night, broken only by the tinkling of the hunter's bell and the scampering feet of the frightened deer. The upper part of the picture is simply but beautifully composed with a broad, winding river, a thick clump of trees, and the starlit sky ; the dark, heavy foliage massed against the sky, and the silver-grey reflection on the water. Rocks and stunted shrubs and a suggestion of a mountain stream fill up the foreground. The picture is painted in a very low key, but the colour is luminous and full of atmosphere ; there is a beautiful sentiment in the whole design, like Mozart's music in its limpid, flowing melody.

The art of the Moguls was not suppressed by the interdicts of Aurangzīb, and did not die with the Mogul dynasty, for though, like our modern art, it was divorced from religion and regarded by the Court only as a distraction and amusement, it was grafted upon the older Buddhist and Hindu schools, upon a truly Indian tradition which was never uprooted, and continued to flourish long after the glory of the Moguls had departed.

Throughout the stormy period of the eighteenth century and even under the depressing influences of the nineteenth Indian artists and craftsmen could create things of beauty recalling the strength and spiritual fervour of former days, and there still survive painters following the old traditions who, but for the generally vitiated taste of the " educated " classes in India, would be honoured as artists of distinction were under Hindu and Mogul rule.

Plate LXVI, " Travellers round a Camp-fire," is a late eighteenth-century work of an unknown artist, possibly a descendant of the painter of the Bagh fresco (Plate LII), who in a different milieu recorded his impression of Indian life as faithfully as his ancestor did in the old Buddhist vihara. A party of travellers is seated round a blazing fire—painted in gold—in the compound of a *dharmsāla*, a native rest-house. The artist has been attracted by the effect of the firelight in the darkness, and with the simplicity and directness of true genius he has given a wonderful

PLATE LXV

DEER–HUNTING BY NIGHT

" impression " of it—what Whistler would have called a symphony in black, gold, and green. We see some figures in the full glare of the firelight placed in bold relief against the darkness of the night ; others silhouetted against the blaze ; the reflection on the walls, the trunks, and lower branches of the trees ; the flash on the window and under the eaves of the house ; the ghostly shadows and the depths of the all-environing gloom, relieved by the glimmer of the starlit sky.

Everyone familiar with Indian mofussil life will recognise the truthfulness of the native types given with such intense concentration and dramatic skill. The young man, half in shadow, telling a story ; the old man with a sleeping child on his lap, and the two old men with whom he is conversing—one smoking a hookah, the other resting with his hand under his chin, are all masterpieces of characterisation.

The original of Plate LXVII, which may be somewhat earlier in date than the last, gives a more familiar aspect of Indian art, for here we have a rendering of daylight with the full strength of the Indian painter's palette, when he revels in the glow and warmth of tropical sunshine. It suggests a *motif* for the decoration of the *chitrasāla* of an Indian garden-house, which must have been as delightful as a Pompeian villa when its walls were adorned like this, and not disfigured with vulgar modern gewgaws.

In its unfinished state the picture illustrates the painter's method of work.

The centre of the picture is filled by three young and high-born Muhammadan ladies—whose fair and finely chiselled features are drawn with a Botticellian grace, sitting by the side of a lotus-pool, taking refreshments and conversing gaily. Unobserved and at their ease in the seclusion of the zanana garden, they have thrown aside their veils and are cooling their feet in the water. The necessary floral ornaments of the pool, the lotus-flowers, are left unpainted, as well as some of the details of dress. Under the shade of the trees behind another fair lady with a dusky Hindu companion are standing ; an attendant bringing wine or rose-water finishes up the group. There is no suggestion of individual portraiture, as in most Mogul composition, but a fine feeling for rhythmic line and harmonious spatial design.

The form and structure of the trees are explained with breadth and simplicity as a foundation for the finishing touches which are wanting. The vivid contrasts of pure colour, laid on uncompromisingly without softening or half-tones, give the warmth and brightness of an Indian atmosphere and help to sustain the dominant note of youthful vivacity and enjoyment.

" A Music Party," Plate LXVIII, is an example of the popular art of the nineteenth century, founded on the old traditions, which has nearly

PLATE LXVI

TRAVELLERS ROUND A CAMP-FIRE

succumbed to the debasing influences of modern
Indian life. There is an artistic quality in this
picture which, in spite of the crudeness of the
drawing, gives it a far higher value than any
of the Anglicised and commercialised Indian
art, sometimes more sophisticated and preten-
tious, but always insincere, which is supplant-
ing it.

Like the pure melody of an old folk-song, it is
a true creation of national sentiment, of the poetic
impulse which flows spontaneously from the
heart of a people inspired by the joy of life and
love of beauty. In the previous illustrations we
have seen how an Indian artist shows the " gloom
of gloom"; here we have the " sunshine of
sunshine," given with the same pure delight with
which the lark trills his song of joy in the high
heavens on a summer morning. The figures in
the picture are by no means attractive types,
or very deeply studied as to character ; but their
glowing draperies and the gay colours of the
musical instruments, together with the pearly
whiteness of the marble and the bright hues of
the flowers, serve the purpose of the artist—to
express the beauty and gladness of the radiant
Indian sunlight.

And, just as in Indian music there are no com-
plicated harmonies, but a subtle flow of pure
intensive melody, so in painting, too, the Indian
artist eschews strong shadows and broken colours,

17

producing an effect of light and atmosphere by the perfect rhythm of his colour-music.

In all Indian paintings, when the art is spontaneous and unaffected, the very Indian qualities of infinite patience and perfect self-control are strongly manifested. Patience unlimited is bestowed upon detail, apparently the most insignificant, which the artist values, but everything is rigorously excluded which he thinks foreign to his purpose. There is no self-advertisement, no cheap effects to attract the applause of the ignorant, no vulgar trickery or playing to the gallery. This restraint and self-control the inartistic mind, accustomed to the loud self-assertion and aggressive realism of common modern painting, often mistakes for defective power of expression.

A Japanese writer of the eighteenth century, quoted by Dr. Anderson, gives a very keen criticism of the realistic tendency of modern European art. " It is the fault of foreign pictures that they dive too deeply into realities, and preserve many details that were better suppressed. . . . Such works are but groups of words. The Japanese picture should be a poem of form and colour." [1]

It is just in this different idea of realism and different outlook upon nature that we find the gulf which separates Eastern art from the aca-

[1] " Pictorial Arts of Japan," vol. ii, p. 242.

PLATE LXVII

IN A ZANANA GARDEN

PLATE LXVII

IN A ZANANA GARDEN

مجنون در آغوش لیلی

demic art of Europe. The difference which the European and Anglicised Indian attributes to defective technical powers or undeveloped intellect, is really due to a different intellectual atmosphere and a different artistic temperament, created by the different answers which East and West give to the question—what is reality ?

It is chiefly because the modern European usually refuses to recognise anything which is not evident to his own perceptive faculties that he finds the difference so irreconcilable and the gulf so impassable. The Indian artist lives in a world of his own imagination, where the stolid Anglo-Saxon is unable to follow him ; but until the Western pedagogue brought Indian culture into contempt and stifled the inherited artistic instincts of Indian youth with his own pedantic formulæ, the Indian artist found that his traditional methods were perfectly adequate for obtaining that response from his public which every artist needs.

It is one of the characteristics of a healthy national art that the artist has no need of vulgar extraneous efforts to make himself appreciated by his public. He is the exponent of national art culture, not a specialist shut up in a narrow domain of knowledge from which the world at large is excluded. Therefore he can be sure that a suggestion of his own thought-impressions will evoke a response from his public, just as a note of music finds a response in every wire tuned to the same pitch through which the vibration passes. Relying on his knowledge of sympathetic response from his public, he develops his representation of the natural facts and phenomena which form the framework of his art just to the point at which he knows it will communicate to others the exact impression of his own mind, and does not attempt a laboured and superfluous explanation of irrelevant facts. The imagination of the public he is addressing supplies the complement of the imagination of the artist.

Since the pernicious principles of the Italian Renaissance, the bigotry of Puritanism, and the pedantry of pseudo-classical education combined to destroy the national art of Europe, the public has demanded from the artist not imagination and ideas, but facts—archæological, historical, biographical or otherwise, relevant or irrelevant— only facts which it can understand. When an imaginative artist appears he must now address an unimaginative public through a middleman, an art critic, who explains as best he can in words what the artist intends to convey with his pencil, brush, or chisel, so that society, which does not like to confess itself Philistine, may talk glibly of what it does not know or feel.

Art limps badly upon these literary crutches, and in the artificial conditions of modern life there is no longer that mutual understanding

PLATE LXVIII.

A MUSIC PARTY

PLATE LXVIII

A MUSIC PARTY

between the artist and his public which existed when art was a popular language of much greater intellectual and moral influence than mere book-learning. The curse of our false classicism, so utterly inconsistent with the true spirit of ancient culture, now hangs heavy upon the national art of India, and the educated Indian, trained in the sordid and squalid atmosphere of Indian universities, becomes completely out of touch with his own national artistic thought, and attributes to Indian art the defects which should properly be ascribed to his own lack of artistic development.

The next two illustrations, Plates LXIX and LXX, show how Indian artists in the early days of British rule, before schools of art imposed their pedantic recipes upon them, were employed by their European masters, as their ancestors had been employed at the Court of the Great Mogul. This occupation has been lost to them by the development of photography and by the changed conditions of Anglo-Indian life, which give greater opportunities for the employment of European portrait-painters, but have certainly not raised the standard of public taste. At the same time the spread of the belief in the inferiority of Indian art, which English education does so much to foster, has taken away from Indian portrait-painters the patronage of their wealthier countrymen.

These interesting drawings of Anglo-Indian

burra-sahibs and *mem-sahibs* as they lived in Bengal in Georgian times were presented to the Calcutta Art Gallery by Dr. Abanindra Nath Tagore, C.I.E. They were found in the possession of a native artist of Calcutta, one of whose ancestors, Gulab Lal, was employed at the Mogul Court about the year 1719, in the reign of Muhammad Shah. Though lacking the wonderful finesse of the best Mogul miniaturists they are of considerable artistic merit and give very amusing glimpses into the Anglo-Indian life of the period.

They were probably executed by one of the same family who was working at Murshidabad in the employ of the Nawab Nazim of Bengal, about 1782. The living representative of this artist family, when I discovered him, had been obliged, from want of encouragement for his art, to give up the profession of a miniature painter, and to look for more remunerative employment in drawing patterns for a European firm which imported Manchester piece-goods. He has now an appointment as teacher in the Calcutta School of Art.

The condition of most other descendants of the great artists of the Mogul Courts is an equally painful commentary on the decadence of fine art in India. There are still a few at Delhi and Agra who find employment at photographic establishments, or in painting the well-known miniatures on ivory which are bought by tourists

PLATE LXIX

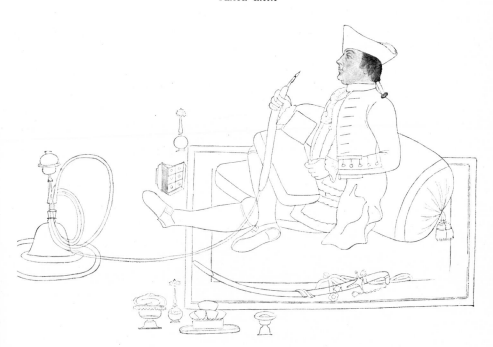

PORTRAIT OF AN ANGLO-INDIAN OF THE GEORGIAN PERIOD

PLATE LXX

PORTRAITS OF ANGLO-INDIANS OF THE GEORGIAN PERIOD

(From drawings by a native artist in the Calcutta Art Gallery)

as Indian "curiosities." A few of the Indian Princes continue to employ court painters of the old school, though it is considered unprogressive to do so. If they take any practical interest in art it nearly always means that the painters are sent to Europe or to an Indian school of art, so that all the Indian traditions they have inherited may be uprooted.

There is, however, in India a not inconsiderable survival of genuine folk-art and of the fine traditions of the temple artist-craftsman, which, if Indians were to take an intelligent and serious interest in them, would be the surest foundation on which to build up the revival of Indian painting. But neither the teaching of schools of art nor that of the universities seems likely to stimulate greatly public interest in art, except as a hobby for the collector or as a plaything for the politician.

CHAPTER IV

THE FUTURE OF INDIAN ART

IN the foregoing summary review of Indian sculpture and painting, I have endeavoured to indicate,
by the aid of some of those masterpieces, unfortunately few, which have been salved from the
wreckage of a great civilisation and culture, the
principal psychological impulses through which
the ideals of Indian fine art were created. We
have seen first an epoch inspired by intense
religious fervour, analogous to the Romanesque
and Gothic epochs of European art, in which the
Indian people, dissatisfied with philosophical ab-
stractions and yearning for tangible symbols of
their spiritual desires and beliefs, used the
means provided for them by an alien faith and
art—just as the early Christians adopted the art
of pagan Greece and Rome. Gradually the Indian
consciousness, asserting itself more strongly,
evolved its own artistic ideals—ideals as different
from the original foreign types as Gothic art
differs from Roman—and thus created that Indian

art which gave its inspiration to the æsthetic thought of all Asia.

The illustrations of some of the masterpieces of that great epoch of religious art, and the explanation given, have been, I hope, sufficient to show that the ideals thus realised were not, as some archæologists aver, the result of the feeble efforts of undeveloped artistic powers to imitate decadent types of the Hellenic school, but original, imaginative conceptions which, rightly understood, are worthy to rank with the noblest conceptions of the West.

After many centuries, when the spiritual fervour which had created the classic art of Ajantā, Ellora, and Borobudur ran riot in a maze of elaborate ritual in which religious symbolism usurped the function of the artist's creative mind, Indian imagination began to spend its vital force in a repetition of æsthetic formularies to which all the virtue of the Brahman's mantras was attached. Yet even in this jungle of exuberant ritualism a great tradition maintained itself, and much noble art towered over the tangled undergrowth, which reformers like Sankarāchārya tried to cut away—the temples of the Cholas with their Natārājas, and the great cities of the north, Mathurā, Kanauj, and Somnath, whose unrivalled beauty and magnificence excited the cupidity and admiration of Mahmūd of Ghazni.

The Muhammadan conquest brought into India another clash of ideals, a puritanical movement, in which the fine arts were banished from places of worship, and an orgy of reckless destruction began, through which the followers of Islam, like to Puritans of Europe, hoped vainly that human nature could be purged of hypocrisy, worldliness, and superstition. Indian sculpture and painting under the influence of Islam was limited to a very narrow range ; the effect of the restriction in emasculating architectural sculpture can be seen in northern India to-day. But though the vision of the artist was thus limited, the instinct for artistic creation did not wither, the old craft traditions renewed their life in working out new problems of construction and design. Thus the Hindu genius in the service of Islam created a noble idealistic architecture, and, under the enlightened patronage of Akbar, a secular school of Indian painting arose, which, though it lacked the high spiritual purpose which inspired the old religious schools, nevertheless deserves the appreciation and careful study of all artists for its perfect sincerity and high technical distinction—qualities which are conspicuously wanting in the degenerate Anglicised art of the present day.

I think my illustrations will show that when the Indian artist finds himself on the same plane of thought as the European he does not lack the capacity for drawing correctly, according to academic rules, or for making truthful transcripts from Nature.

Hindu painters, even when working in the narrow groove of the Mogul Court, did not quite forget that art has a higher aim, to penetrate the soul of things and to bring us into closer relation with Nature's eternal verities. But when art gave up its birthright as the ethical teacher and spiritual helper of mankind, only to minister to the vanity and self-indulgence of the wealthy and indolent ; when man ceased to use his highest creative faculties in the daily worship of his Creator, the Decadence, miscalled in Europe the Renaissance, had already begun. India's loss of spiritual power is the measure of the degradation of her art.

When at last India began to emerge from the political chaos of the eighteenth century and all its attendant miseries, the fine arts not only ceased to have the encouragement of state patronage which had been so lavishly bestowed upon them by the Great Moguls, but the idea that the Indian intellect had always been artistically inferior to the European penetrated the whole fabric of art creation like dry rot. The unimaginative Anglo-Saxon succeeded the imaginative Mogul in the sovereignty of India, and the people, distracted by long years of anarchy, accepted the change gladly. We have fulfilled our duties as policemen, and take a just pride in the organisation, peace, and security which we have substituted for chaos, bloodshed, and general brigandage. It is not a small thing, as Sir Mountstuart Grant-Duff said in one of his Elgin addresses, " to keep the peace between 250,000,000 of men." But it was inevitable that our success in this direction should lead to even greater responsibilities being thrust upon us. The East came to learn the wisdom of the West, and *nolens volens* we have been compelled to undertake the much more difficult duties of teacher and spiritual adviser, as well as those of policemen.

The critic who endeavoured to form a just estimate of the results we have achieved in the two former capacities would naturally take into consideration the present condition of art in India, for as a symptom of intellectual, moral, and spiritual progress the condition of a national art is a more certain guide than any blue books or statistics. Such a critic would perhaps be inclined to regard the degeneration and decay of Indian art, which have certainly been much more rapid under the peace and security of British rule than under the most chaotic period of native government, as a very unfavourable indication—and, so far as it goes, it may be regarded as such. But it may be that this seemingly inexplicable decay in spite of the blessings of order and settled government which

PLATE LXXI

KĀCHA AND DEVĀJĀNI

(A fresco painting by Abanindra Nath Tagore)

we have conferred upon the country is due to causes which, in process of time, may be removed. One of the most conspicuous of these causes is the pernicious example we have held up in Anglo-Indian art, more especially in the architecture of public buildings—always the outward and visible sign of the inner civic consciousness.

If art is the mirror of the age, it must always be humiliating to any artistic Englishman to contemplate our make-believe Gothic and Classic cathedrals, churches, colleges, schools, offices of state, and historical monuments, and compare their banality, ugliness, and squalor with the dignity, strength, and fine craftsmanship of the splendid monuments of the Mogul Empire. It must be equally humiliating to any artistic Indian to find his educated fellow-countrymen imposed upon by these deplorable makeshifts, and using them as models instead of the great master-pieces of their own national architecture.

But when all these things are seen in their true perspective the future historian of British India will be able to find, even in our blunders, sufficient evidence of high endeavour and moral earnest-ness. We live in an age of transition, and in India the ideals of two great civilisations are now in the melting-pot—the dross will accumulate on the surface, but when that is cleared away the pure gold that is in both will be found beneath. The art of present and past generations of Anglo-

Indians reveals the dross ; we may hope that the art of the New India which is forming will show the precious metal.

At a time when our own national education was miserably defective, and when our own national art had lost all its vitality and sincerity, we undertook to hold up the torch of European civilisation and progress in the East. And of the two statesmen, Bentinck and Macaulay, who laid the foundations of Western Education in India, the first considered Indian art so lightly that he was only diverted from selling the Tāj Mahall for the value of its marble because the proceeds of a test auction of materials from the Agra Palace proved unsatisfactory, and the second did not hesitate to declare his conviction, after an absurdly inadequate acquaintance with India, that the whole of Indian and Arabic literature was not worth a single bookshelf of a good European library. *Tempora mutantur*, and it is now largely due to the work and appreciation of European scholars and men of letters that New India has been aroused to undertake for herself researches into the priceless stores of oriental literature which had been so long neglected. What we have not yet accomplished is the proper application of our improved knowledge of Indian culture and civilisation to the administrative work of the Empire, especially in matters of education.

The great problems of education in India, which should command Great Britain's highest statesmanship and best intellect, have generally since Macaulay's time been relegated to the pedagogic specialist, often narrow and provincial in his views, and as a rule entirely out of touch with real Indian life and thought.

The statesman has not yet appeared to organise an Indian university affording to Indian youth the best fruits of both Eastern and Western culture, and fit to be a successor of the great universities of Buddhist and Hindu rule in stimulating the national artistic genius—that creative power of the people in the exercise of which will always be found one of the surest guarantees for national prosperity and contentment.

The late Dr. A. C. Benson, Master of Magdalene College, Cambridge, in a trenchant criticism of public school education in England, condemned

" the intellectual tyranny that sits enthroned in the centre, a monopoly sustained by specialists, a despotic, inelastic, devastating theory. It is the foe of liberality of thought, mental expansion, intellectual progress, because it substitutes for the intellectual spirit a small and minute image of its own devising. . . . For the majority of boys the classical system, simply because it is the rigid application of a very special subject to the mental needs of an infinite variety of minds, is not only no education at all, but a deliberate sterilisation of the intellectual seed-plot, a perverse maltreatment of the ingenuous mind."

These words, *mutatis mutandis*, may be taken as very applicable to our system of higher education in India ; only the evil of it is there intensely aggravated because Indian students are practically denied any other means of education than the university courses. Our universities have always stood in the eyes of India as representative of the best light and leading of the West ; yet the disabilities and injuries which they, as exponents of all learning recognised by the State, inflict upon Indian art and industry are incalculable, for not only do they refuse to allow art its legitimate place in the mental and moral equipment of Indian youth—the average Indian graduate, with all his remarkable assimilative powers, is often less developed artistically than a Pacific islander —but by practically excluding all Indian artists of the old hereditary professions from the honours and emoluments of state employment, they lower the status of Indian art and give a wholly unjustifiable preference to the art imported from Europe, which comes with the prestige of a presumed higher order of civilisation. The building of New Delhi has demonstrated on a grand scale how " the sterilisation of the intellectual seed-plot " by the universities is withering the roots of Indian art and craft.

It is only necessary to compare the present
position of Indian artists with that of their fore-
fathers to see the evil our whole administrative
system works upon art in India. In the time of
Akbar, Jahāngīr, and Shah Jahān the best artists
became grandees of the Court and sometimes
intimate friends of the Emperor himself. In
Rajputana also, under Hindu rule, painters and
architects held dignified positions at Court, and
besides liberal pecuniary rewards they were often
given special honours and grants of land. In the
Imperial Library at Calcutta there is preserved a
Persian manuscript giving the names of the
designers and chief constructors of the Tāj Mahall
and the salaries they received. The three principal designers were each paid a thousand rupees a
month ; another received eight hundred ; six
others four hundred ; and nine others from two
hundred to four hundred a month. These salaries
would represent a considerably larger sum in
present Indian currency. But the descendants
of these men in India, who practise their professions now with little less ability, though their
opportunities for exercising it under our Public
Works system are miserably few, are considered
well paid at thirty, forty, or sixty rupees a month.

The question of remuneration or reward is not,
however, a vital one. The best Indian artists
are often content with a pittance when the work
they do is religiously inspired. The modern

18

bureaucratic machine cannot use them as artists, however lavishly it spends : it can only find a place for them as dull mechanics and discontented artisans.

Neither the building of the Victoria Memorial at Calcutta nor the building of New Delhi with a colossal expenditure has brought better opportunities or rewards for Indian artists. None have been employed in these two great projects, except in a subordinate capacity to copy the paper patterns of the European experts and to fix up sculptures and paintings made in London studios which must be totally irrelevant to Indian art and Indian life.

Elegant exercises in Indian archæology by eminent experts may serve the purpose of appealing to the *amour-propre* of Indian politicians, but they do not advance the art of building either in India or in Europe. The endowment of Chairs of Fine Art in Indian Universities, after the fashion of Oxford and Cambridge ; the establishment of schools of art and architecture in which Indian students can learn the theory and practice of the fine arts, as taught in London and Paris, and the patronage of Indian artists by sympathetic Governors and high officials, do nothing to alter the bureaucratic system which is destroying root and branch the traditions of art in India. They only tend to obscure the vital issues and to create an atmosphere of make-believe which is more harmful in its influence than a policy of absolute *laissez-faire*.

If we adopted a purely Philistine attitude, declaring that our mission was to set an example of what we are proud to call plain, practical, British common sense, we should at least be consistent and straightforward. Or if we avowed that our task in India was only to protect the down-trodden pariah ; to remove the barriers by which a selfish and corrupt hierarchy has prevented the intellectual and social advancement of the lower orders ; to free the ryot from the bondage of the sowcar ; to purify the administration and to hold the scales of justice even— we might perhaps view with a quiet conscience the continuous degradation of Indian art which we do not seriously attempt to arrest.

But this is not our attitude. We pose as apostles of higher culture, as patrons of art and letters, and exponents of a superior order of civilisation ; and by so doing we have persuaded educated Indians and the aristocracy of the country, who are the principal patrons of art, to leave their artistic consciences in our keeping, to adopt the models we approve of, and to aim at the ideals at which we profess to aim.

We should not, then, introduce into Indian civic life a standard of art immeasurably inferior to its own—the contractor's art and the jerry-builder are our æsthetic importations ; we should not

affect to consider art as a proper moral influence
for Indian jails and reformatories and shut it out
of the universities ; and if we argue that the
indifference to Indian art of the India we have
educated is a proof that it does not really interpret the Indian mind, we should at least be sure
that we are better able to interpret it ourselves.
You cannot know a people's mind if you do not
understand their art.

We certainly do, as a rule, take a more sincere
interest in Indian art than most "educated"
Indians, but it is generally a purely academic and
archæological interest ; and it is quite natural
and almost inevitable that it should be so. Many
English and Anglo-Indian drawing-rooms have
more or less unpractical Indian furniture, and
various useless ornaments which we call Indian
curiosities. At times we make spasmodic and
ill-considered attempts to encourage Indian art
by holding exhibitions of this class of work.
These things simply show how far we are from
appreciating the vital points of the question,
how little we understand the Indian mind ourselves.

For this is Indian art, spurious and make-
believe like our official architecture, with all the
virtue, all the spirituality, all the love and worship,
all that has made it great and true in the past,
taken out of it. Indian art was born in the
village and nurtured in the pilgrim's camp ; it

can never thrive in the sickly, artificial atmosphere
of the European drawing-room or in a Western
market-place. We have driven it from the great
cities of India. It has no real part in our civic
life, and its last refuge is now in the villages and
towns remote from European influence. But
this last refuge will always be its surest stronghold ; when art in Europe gets back to the
villages the real Renaissance will have begun.
In the villages of India the true artistic spirit
still survives, and if we and " educated " Indians
would know what true Indian art is we must go
there, where the heart of India beats, where the
voices of her dead myriads still are heard, and
learn a lesson that neither London nor Paris can
teach. Some time ago I drew attention, in a
monograph on the stone-carving of Bengal,[1] to
some modern architectural decoration, just as
beautiful in feeling and execution as the carving
of a medieval Gothic Cathedral, done by Orissan
sculptors, the direct descendants of those who
built and sculptured the famous temple of the
Sun-god, already referred to (p. 147). For the
last twenty or thirty years some of them have
been carving the decoration of a temple at Jaipur,
the ancient capital of the province ; their wages,
fourpence a day, are being paid by a religious
mendicant who has spent his whole life in begging
for funds for this purpose.

[1] Bengal Secretarial Book Depot, 1906.

When I suggested that wealthy Bengalis would do better in having such art as this in their houses, rather than tenth-rate commercial Italian statuary, and that Calcutta would gain in many ways if we substituted real Indian sculpture, conceived in this spirit, for foolish Gothic and classic imitations (ten or twenty times more costly), " The Statesman," one of the principal European newspapers of Calcutta, applauded the taste of educated Indians, declaring that it was highly commendable and gratifying to those who believed that the mission of Europe was to awaken Asia and lift her up to the Western level of culture.

" Until Indian art," it asserted sententiously, " has mastered the cardinal secret of simplicity; until the Indian artists have begun to understand the meaning of large effects; until abandoning mere amplification they prove capable of a conception of an organic whole, the products of native art are bound to remain in the state of arrested growth they have been all these thousands of years."

The abysmal ignorance of Indian art-history revealed in the last sentence may be pardoned, for it is not confined to the editorial columns of Anglo-Indian newspapers; but what are these " large effects," these Parnassian heights, seemingly inaccessible to ourselves, which we would fain make others climb? When we have

THE END OF THE JOURNEY

(Painted by Abanindra Nath Tagore)

succeeded in creating in India, either by our own exertions or through the Indian intellect, anything ethically or æsthetically as great as a medieval Gothic Cathedral we may begin to aim at something higher. But all such academic recipes, relating either to art, architecture, or general education, are just as vain and useless as the *mantras* of uncomprehended mysteries the Tibetan lama drones as he twirls his praying-wheel.

Europeans now collect Indian pictures enthusiastically and critics generally take a much more sympathetic attitude towards Indian art than they did twenty years ago ; but the view that the salvation of Indian art lies only in the application of the academic nostrums of Europe still has the weight of official influence behind it. If the spirit of the present Prime Minister's eloquent appeal for the revival of English village craftsmanship[1] were applied to administrative problems in India, there would be no reason to confine our sympathy and admiration for Indian art to the great monuments of antiquity. The drying up of the living springs of craftsmanship is a more grievous loss to India than the ruin of all her ancient monuments.

Change there must be in Indian art ; that is both inevitable and necessary, for there is no real life in an art which never changes. But the

[1] Published by the Royal Society of Arts, 1927.

change must come from the quickening, not from
the deadening, of the creative faculties ; from the
stimulating of thought and the strenuous up-
holding of higher ideals, not from the substitution
of one academic formula for another.

The rank materialism which is the basis of the
modern Indian university system tends to produce
in the Indian mind the same attitude towards
art that is characteristic of the average European
university man. In this view, so contrary to all
the laws of nature and all the experience of
the human race, art is one of those luxuries which
may be enjoyed when other intellectual and all
bodily wants are satisfied ; but at the same time
it is to be considered as the most easily dispensed
with of all intellectual stimulants, and as having
no practical bearing on the intellectual growth or
spiritual life of the average human being. It is
enough for the Indian undergraduate that it
counts for nothing in the university examinations,
and in after-life he is quite content to accept the
common formularies which regulate the prevailing
fashions as representing his correct attitude
towards art.

In 1905, when the reform of the Calcutta
University was under discussion, a scheme for
giving art design a definite place in the curriculum
by the side of science, drawn up by myself and
accepted by the Faculty of Arts after full discussion, was suppressed without comment by Lord

Curzon's committee at Simla. Since then, through the efforts of the late Sir Ashutosh Mukerjee, a Chair of Indian Fine Art has been created.

As regards the government schools of art, originally established to bring the fine arts of the West to the benighted East, the European directors do not now affect to despise Indian art : they profess to admire it, but attempt to justify their position as teachers by the argument that there are certain fundamental principles common to the art of all countries, which the traditional artists of India do not understand and cannot teach, and therefore the renaissance of art in India must be effected by leading Indian students to the faithful study of nature, through the paraphernalia and technique of modern European academies.

Now if Europe and Asia had both failed to produce the highest art before this academic system was evolved ; if modern universities created poets and modern ateliers created artists, there might be some logic in the argument. But this is not the case. Poets sometimes emerge alive from the university mill ; artists occasionally pass through academic courses of instruction without complete atrophy of their imaginative faculties. But no one can maintain that owing to this academic system modern European literature and art stand higher than they did in pre-Renaissance days.

In India, where the system has been followed, more or less efficiently, for seventy years, it has been destructive of all artistic vitality. No modern Indian portrait-painter, led to the faithful study of nature as understood by European artists, can be put into the same class with the Mogul Court painters who followed their own traditions. The mural paintings of Government House, Bombay,[1] the latest and technically, perhaps, the best products of the system, are a facile parody of Leighton's fresco of " The Arts of Peace " in the Victoria and Albert Museum, but they are neither Indian nor true to nature and far inferior as decorative art to the unsophisticated work of a nineteenth-century Kangra painter. A European artist, viewing these paintings with indulgence and condescension, might find much merit in them as the work of promising Indian schoolboys, but only if he does not know or care to learn the end of the story—these clever school-boys never grow up ! Therein lies the damnable defect of the whole system. Mother India may be in many ways inefficient and behind the times, but in the upbringing of her own children as artists she has nothing to learn from modern Europe.

The formula of the Royal Academy curriculum from which this school of painting has its acknow-ledged source makes Indian ploughmen, gardeners,

[1] Illustrated in " Apollo," July, 1927.

and basket-makers limp like antique statues and
go about their work in Leightonesque poses, so
that certain wall spaces in Government House
may be decoratively treated. The architects
of New Delhi, who as universal providers were
commissioned to restore the arts of the Empire,
commend these paintings and propose that the
same rhythmical formula, which can easily be
adjusted to all the races of mankind, as an
ingenious rhymester turns out limericks, shall
be taught in an Imperial School of Design at
Delhi by European masters who have acquired
"reputations in a world-arena," so that Macaulay's ideal of education may be realised and the
New Delhis of the future may be decorated, if
not built, by Indians drilled in thinking imperially.
This, as Dr. A. C. Benson would have said, is not
art or education, but a perverse maltreatment
of the ingenuous mind.

Unfortunately art and education in India are
mixed up and confused with political issues. If
India had no living traditions of her own, and
her own culture had never risen higher than
that of Africa, Australia, or Canada, the gospel of
Imperialism preached by the architects of New
Delhi, and the threadbare formulæ of European
ateliers, might satisfy the ideals of New India
by opening up careers for the literate classes
hitherto almost monopolised by European experts. But a policy which starts from placing

Indians on an artistic level with the uncivilised races of mankind, and refuses to utilise to the fullest extent the capacities of living Indian craftsmen ; which views complacently the drying up of the springs of Indian craftsmanship if only British craftsmanship may exhibit its superiority, does not show political wisdom or educational insight.

The recent political reforms have placed the responsibility for art administration in India in the hands of English-educated Indians, few of whom have yet shown a firmer grasp of India's artistic problems than their predecessors in office, who, if art did not happen to be their own special hobby, left the solution of them to the personal inclinations of European practitioners. New India, in matters of taste, is now split into two camps, one of which hails the propaganda of the Bombay School as the modern revelation of art to educated India, and the other which follows the lead of Dr. Abanindra Nath Tagore, the founder of the new Calcutta School of Painting.

Dr. Tagore, the artist-poet of Bengal, is not unrecognised " in the world-arena," for exhibitions of his work and of the considerable band of pupils he has gathered round him have not only established one of the most interesting social events in Calcutta, but have won high appreciation from many of the best art critics of Paris, Berlin, and London. Though well-educated in the European

PLATE LXXIV

SIVA-SĪMANTINĪ

(Painted by Abanindra Nath Tagore)

sense, Dr. Tagore never came within the depressing æsthetic environment of an Indian University, and very speedily gave up the European routine of technical training which was his starting-point as an artist. Having thus escaped the Scylla and Charybdis upon which so many Indian art students have been wrecked, he devoted himself to a close study of the Indian pictures which I was then collecting for the Government Art Gallery, and this collection was the guiding influence in his artistic development, though in matters of technique he has adopted a compromise between European and Indian methods.

Dr. Tagore's æsthetic outlook is not, however, narrowed down to any particular school or formula : he can fully appreciate all that is best in European art, ancient and modern, without sinking his own personality in the bog of internationalism. His art is Indian, but his own. Circumstances over which they had no control have prevented Dr. Tagore and his fellow-artists from rising to " imperial " heights as mural painters. My own efforts, as Principal of the Calcutta School of Art, were directed towards finding for his remarkable genius the widest scope in mural decoration. One of his earliest efforts was an essay in Indian *fresco buono*, Plate LXXI, illustrating the story of Kācha and Devājāni from the Mahābhārata. He also, on my advice, began the preparation of a series of cartoons for the decoration of the Government Art Gallery in fresco, but the scheme was dropped after my retirement, the Public Works Department not being interested in the revival of Indian art. Lord Curzon, whose interest in Indian art was only archæological, made the decoration of the Victoria Memorial an imperial reserve which Indian artists were not allowed to enter, apparently because the Victorian era did not recognise Indian sculpture and painting as fine art. The architects of New Delhi also make art only a matter of taste, of which they are the final arbiters, and exclude those who do not conform to their imperial prescription. Unless, therefore, the traditions of the old *chitra-sālas* should be revived by Indians themselves, through a sincere interest in the future of their own art, the only resource left to Indian painters is to adapt themselves to their environment by working on a diminutive scale like the Mogul painters, who likewise appealed only to an exclusive coterie of the intelligentsia.

As painters in miniature, however, the artists of the New School owe much to the lively interest and support of the European community of Calcutta, both official and non-official. The Indian Society of Oriental Art, of which Sir John Woodroffe was the leading spirit, was started in 1907 with the object of giving them encouragement, and has since become an important centre of friendly co-operation between East and West in the field of Art. Two Governors of Bengal, the late Lord Carmichael and Lord Ronaldshay, who were patrons of the Society, gave the New School the most effective official help.

Lord Ronaldshay himself, in an article printed in the " Asiatic Review," [1] on the history and significance of this art revival in Bengal, gives details of the practical aid which the Government of Bengal afforded the school started by Dr. Tagore in 1916, with the co-operation of his gifted brother, Mr. Goganendra Nath Tagore, and his uncle, the poet. A Government grant enabled it to secure suitable accommodation for a studio and lecture hall :

" Eminent exponents of the new school were engaged as teachers, and scholarships for indigent pupils were provided. A series of lectures was planned, and the publication of an art journal under the title of ' Rūpam ' (Form) arranged for. This reorganisation was explained at a gathering held at Government House on December 4th, 1919, at which recent works of a number of the artists of the new school were on view, and an address, in part descriptive and in part critical of the new movement, was given by Mr. O. C. Gangoly, himself an accomplished artist and a discerning art critic. . . . First and foremost he described the work of the school as consciously

[1] July 1924.

and intentionally idealistic. It was the avowed intention of its masters, he declared, to escape from ' the photographic vision and to secure an introspective outlook on things which takes one away from the material objectives of life to a rarefied atmosphere of beauty and romance.' And he went on to lay emphasis on the characteristic of the movement. Its exponents, ' instead of busying themselves with recording the superficial aspects of phenomena, have worked with a deeper motive and a profounder suggestion, seeking to wean the human mind from the obvious and the external reality of the senses, disdaining to imitate nature for its own sake, and striving to find significant forms to suggest the formless infinity which is hidden behind the physical world of forms.' They have sought, that is to say, to maintain the distinctive and essential characteristic of the art of India, namely, its extreme idealism."

In answer to the question, what is the significance attaching to the movement ? Lord Ronaldshay writes :

" It was an awakening race-consciousness expressing itself in terms of art that caused the brothers Tagore to sever their connection with the Government School of Art, and to turn to the cultural traditions and ideals of their own land. . . . Running like a thread through the varying forms of unrest with which India is tormented is a spirit of revolt, sometimes conscious, sometimes subconscious, against the denationalisation

of a proud and sensitive people. Many Indians
have proclaimed this identity of motive behind
varying manifestations of Indian nationalism.
At a time when I was engaged in fighting the
revolutionary movement in Bengal and in supporting the art movement which I have described,
a political writer, whose sympathies were undoubtedly with the former, issued a pamphlet in
which he took this matter as his theme. It was
a reaction against the Westernisation of India,
he declared, that was animating all patriotic
Indians, and in support of his argument that this
same leaven was at work in the domain of literature and art he pointed to the rise of the Tagore
School. ' In Bengal,' he wrote, ' the national
spirit is seeking to satisfy itself in art ; and for
the first time since the decline of the Moghuls a
new school of national art is developing itself—
the school of which Abanindra Nath Tagore is the
founder and master.' "

The New School of Calcutta, therefore, though
cramped in its early growth by Lord Curzon's
æsthetic predilections, owes much to Lord Ronaldshay's broader views of art and statesmanship :
unfortunately they were not effective in imperial
concerns, nor had he the opportunity given to
Lord Hardinge for removing the departmental
impediments which block the main outflow of
Indian artistic energy and add to Indian unrest.
The direct contribution to art of the New Calcutta
School has been considerable and important, but

19

its influence on the future of Indian art will probably be still more felt indirectly, through its teaching. As an inspiring teacher, both in his own school and as Professor of Fine Arts in the Calcutta University, Dr. Tagore has had a wonderful success in re-fertilising the soil made sterile for the best part of a century by a futile academic dogma and in helping future political leaders to understand the fundamental artistic problems with which they have to deal in India.

If the New School has not yet acquired the splendid technique of the old Indian painters, it has certainly revived the spirit of Indian art, and besides invested its work with a charm of true poetry, distinctively its own. Though a protest against denationalisation it represents a happy blending of Eastern and Western thought, from the full realisation of which humanity at large has so much to gain. Mr. Kipling would persuade us that this is an unattainable consummation—a rather insular attitude which can only promote prejudice and misunderstanding.

It is on the technical side that the wrong we have done to Indian art is most apparent and least excusable. It may be difficult to provide in a state educational system, especially under Indian conditions, that intellectual and spiritual stimulus without which no real art can ever be developed. Emerson has truly said that art does not come at the call of a legislature—neither

PLATE LXXV

THE TRIAL OF THE PRINCES

(Painted by Nanda Lal Bose)

can a legislature entirely suppress it merely by neglecting to take cognisance of the artistic faculties. But nothing can excuse the crushing out of all the splendid artistry, of the technical lore and skill of hand inherited from former generations—one of the most valuable industrial assets India possesses—simply from the want of an intelligent adaptation of official machinery for making use of it.

The New School of Calcutta opens up a brighter prospect for the future, but as Professor Lethaby has said, no art that is only one-man deep is worth much. It should be a thousand men deep. Whichever school of pictorial art most accurately interprets the mind of modern India, it is politicians, rather than artists or art-teachers, who control the future of Indian art. For neither painting nor sculpture can be the great and beneficent influence in national life they ought to be when they are both cut off from the roots from which they have sprung, the craftsmanship of building. The effect is the same whether the axe used be of native or foreign make, only when we wield the axe we must not wonder that blame falls upon ourselves.

It remains to be seen whether Indian politicians, handicapped as they are by their Western ideas of art, still possess constructive as well as critical faculties. Will they follow the line of least resistance, that which seems most convenient for departmental routine and themselves, the time-honoured practice of drying up the living springs of craftsmanship in controlling the artistic output of India, or will they apply themselves seriously to the problem of adapting departmental machinery to the needs and conditions of Indian life ? Will they take art as a serious study, or merely as a pleasant relaxation from the cares of office ?

Since the first publication of this book the New Calcutta School has greatly increased its numbers and has now produced three generations of artists of distinction, whose works have been illustrated in the " Modern Review " of Calcutta and in a series of fine monographs edited by Mr. O. C. Gangoly, who also edits " Rūpam," the admirable quarterly review started with Lord Ronaldshay's help, which shows the immense progress, amounting to a revolution, made in the study of æsthetics by the intelligentsia of India in the last twenty years. To these publications I must refer my readers and content myself with the illustration of a few typical works by Dr. Tagore himself and his two pupils, Mr. Nanda Lal Bose, who now directs the art work of Dr. Rabindra Nath Tagore's University at Bolpur, and Mr. Asit Kumar Haldar, Principal of the Government School of Arts and Crafts at Lucknow.

The fresco painting, Plate LXXI, is an early work by Dr. Tagore in which he has expressed with wonderful directness and simplicity the struggle between passion and duty which is the motive of the story. In this and in many other works of the school the fine poetic feeling and depth of expression more than compensate for obvious technical deficiencies. The story is told in the Mahābhārata thus : [1]

There was a supreme contest between the gods and *asuras* for the sovereignty of the three worlds. To control the sacrifices by which the victory would be decided, the gods chose for their priest the sage Vrihaspati ; the *asuras* appointed Sukra as theirs. Sukra knew the secret of reviving the dead, and by his wonderful science restored to life all the enemies of the gods as soon as they were slain. The gods, in despair, begged Kācha, the eldest son of Vrihaspati, to present himself to Sukra as a disciple, so that he might learn from him the mighty secret. Kācha consented and, after taking the vow of discipleship, was received by Sukra. He speedily ingratiated himself in his master's favour, and by singing, dancing, and music won the heart of his fair daughter, Devājāni.

When five hundred years of his discipleship had passed, the *asuras* discovered Kācha's intention, and finding him alone in the woods tending his preceptor's kine they slew him, hacked his body to pieces, and gave them to be devoured

[1] See vol. i, Roy's translation, pp. 232-40.

by wolves and jackals. Sukra, at Devājāni's entreaty, revived him by his magic, but soon afterwards Kācha was again slain by the *asuras* while roaming the forest in search of flowers for the sacrifice. This time they pounded his body into a paste and mixed it with the waters of ocean. But again he was revived by Sukra. Then the *asuras* slew him a third time and burning the body mixed the ashes with the wine Sukra drank.

Devājāni, missing her beloved Kācha, again appealed to her father ; but when Sukra exercised his power and found that Kācha was inside his own body, he cried out, " Oh, Devājāni, Kācha is within me, and there is no way for his coming out alive except by ripping open my own belly ! "

Touched by Devājāni's despair Sukra adopted the only resource left to him—to impart to Kācha his great secret, under a promise that it would be used to restore himself to life as soon as the former was released by Sukra's death. Kācha, beautiful as the full moon, came out of Sukra's belly by ripping it open, and used his newly gained power for the first time in restoring his master to life.

The climax, which Dr. Tagore has taken for his subject, is when Kācha, at the expiration of his vow of discipleship, prepared to return to the abode of the gods. Devājāni, reminding him of her devotion to him, begged of him to fix his

PLATE LXXVI

SATI

" Life of my life, Death's bitter sword
Hath severed us like a broken word :
Rent us in twain who are but one . . .
Shall the flesh survive when the soul is gone ? "

Sarojini Naidu.

affection upon her, and to accept her hand in marriage. But Kācha, regarding their relationship as one which made marriage impossible, exhorted her thus :

" O thou of virtuous vows, do not urge me to such a sinful course ! O thou of fair eyebrows, be kind unto me ! Beautiful one, thou art dearer to me than my preceptor, but the place where thou hast resided in the holy body of Sukra hath also been my abode ! Thou art truly my sister ; therefore, O slender-waisted one, do not speak thus ! Loving one, happily have we passed the days that we have been together. There is perfect sympathy between us. I ask thy leave to return to my abode. Therefore bless me, so that my journey may be safe."

Devājāni, finding her entreaties useless, cursed Kācha, saying : " Since thou dost refuse to make me thy wife when I implore thee, O Kācha, this knowledge thou hast gained shall bear no fruit."

But Kācha replied :

" Curse me, if it please thee. I have told thee the duty of Rishis. I do not deserve thy curse, O Devājāni, but yet thou hast cursed me. Since thou hast done this from passion, not from a sense of duty, thy desire shall not be fulfilled. No Rishi's son shall ever take thy hand in marriage. Thou hast said that my knowledge shall not bear fruit. Let it be so ! *But in him it shall bear fruit to whom I shall impart it.*"

And Kācha departed to the abode of the gods.

Fitzgerald's version of the Rubaiyat of Omar Khayyam has had many illustrators, but none have been quite so successful in reproducing the delicate flavour of the poem as Dr. Tagore in his series of twelve water-colours published by the "Studio" in 1910. Plate LXXII illustrates quatrain XXIX in the first edition :

"Into this Universe, and *why* not knowing,
　Nor *whence*, like Water willy-nilly flowing ;
　　And out of it, as Wind along the Waste,
　I know not *whither*, willy-nilly blowing."

The poet is shown sitting in contemplation by a river's bank, watching the dead leaves blown by the autumn wind as they are carried away by the stream. The subdued twilight tones of the artist's subtle colouring fit very well with the poet's mood, but it is hardly possible to give the finer nuances of the original painting in a reproduction.

"The End of the Journey," Plate LXXIII, which attracted great attention when shown at the exhibition of "Les Orientalistes" in Paris, is an allegory, like the Buddhist *jātakas*, in which animals become partners with humanity in the tragedy and mystery of life. A pack-camel in the desert, worn out and abandoned by its driver, stumbles wearily on a rock and sinks to the ground in its last agony, just as the sun touching the horizon marks the close of day. The crimson glory of the sunset fills the silent sky, while the moans of the dying beast make their pitiful complaint. Dr. Tagore's exquisite feeling interprets the pathos of the scene very finely, filling the spectator with sympathy and a haunting sense of mystery. In technical accomplishment the leader of the modern school is here not far behind the best Mogul animal portrait-painters : as an artistic thinker, or poet, he rises far above them.

In Siva-Sīmantinī (Plate LXXIV) Dr. Tagore treats Hindu mythology with the imagination and fervour of the great Chola artists. Like the Natārāja, Siva-Sīmantinī (" Siva and the Lady ") combines in one person the male and female principle, and in this singularly beautiful conception of a divine incarnation of eternal youth the spiritual ideals of Hinduism have found an artistic interpreter who is modern, in the sense that he is not strictly bound by the canons of Hindu ritual, but yet truly inspired by the highest art traditions of Buddhist and Hindu India.

If circumstances had been different, Mr. Nanda Lal Bose, like his teacher, would have found wider scope for his artistic powers in mural decoration than in book illustration. His strong decorative sense is well shown in " The Trial of the Princes," Plate LXXV, one of a series of coloured illustrations for the Mahābhārata,[1] many of which are admirably adapted for fresco or tempera painting in a public or private *chitra-sāla*. The story as told in the epic is as follows :

Drona, the great master of Yoga and teacher of the Pandava Princes, wishing to test their skill in archery calls them together and, pointing to the target, an artificial bird he has placed on the top of a tree, asks Yudhishthira, the eldest, what he saw. " I see, sir, my brother, the tree and the bird," was the reply. Bidding him stand down, Drona repeated the question and received the same answer from the others until he came to Arjuna, his favourite pupil. " Tell me now, Arjuna, with bow bent, what do you see—the bird, the tree, myself, and your friends ? " " No," said Arjuna, " I see the bird only, neither yourself, nor the tree ! " " Describe the bird," said Drona. " I see only a bird's head," replied Arjuna. " Then shoot," cried Drona, and the next instant the arrow hit the mark and Drona embraced Arjuna with delight as a perfect Yogi in the arts of war.

An earlier work by Mr. Nanda Lal Bose, " Sati," Plate LXXVI, has for its subject the tragedy of Indian wifehood. The young widow, breathing a silent prayer in her last lament, interpreted in Mrs. Sarojini Naidu's beautiful lines, prepares to throw herself upon the funeral pyre of

[1] See " Myths of the Hindus and Buddhists," by Sister Nivedita and Ananda Coomaraswamy (Harrap).

RĀSA LĪLĀ

(Painted by Asit Kumar Haldar)

her dead husband. Mr. Bose, like the Indian poetess, has been inspired by the tender pathos of the scene, rather than by the horror which too often accompanied it.

Mr. Asit Kumar Haldar's range of subject inclines more to the lyrical than the epic mood, but he, like many others of the school, joins the feeling of rhythmic beauty in decoration to real poetic inspiration. He may sometimes offend the academic eye in mere matters of representation, idiosyncrasies found in the work of many great masters. Dr. J. H. Cousins justly observes in his monograph[1] that " to attain to intellectual virtuosity, Mr. Haldar and his fellows would have to shut themselves out from the thrill of Ananda (joy) that appears to flicker through every line of their work."

" Rāsa Līlā," the Dance of Krishna, Plate LXXVII, has technical weaknesses which may jar on delicate academic nerves, but it is beautifully composed and most artists, I venture to think, will join in Dr. Cousins' warm appreciation :

" Ostensibly it is a picture of a moonlight cloud moving across the sky. But superimposed on the cloud is a procession of figures in stately dance. In the centre is Shri Krishna playing on his flute, and before and after are Gopis (his girl-

[1] " Modern Indian Artists," vol. ii (Probsthain & Co.).

companions), drifting with him and with the cloud across the background of night. There is a solemn joy in every lineament of every figure—a spontaneity of chaste delight controlled by some ritual of beauty and truth, which, because it is essential, has no sense of being imposed. We feel that the song of the procession is ' wise and lovely,' as Shelley called the songs of Silenus, notwithstanding the ill-reputation of the sylvan divinity. The loveliness of Mr. Haldar's ' Rāsa Līlā ' is on the face of it. . . . If an artist born in Christian tradition were to paint a picture expressing what is wrapped up in the Hebrew poet's exclamation—' The heavens declare the glory of God and the firmament showeth His handiwork,' he would touch the significance of ' Rāsa Līlā ' with this difference, that to the inner eye of the Indian artist the cloud is not an objective manifestation of a quality of the Creator, but is essentially Himself. Purusha, the Divine energy, gives out the music of his creative desire, and Nature (prakriti) in all the alluring variations of one substance moves rhythmically in response. Our artist, if he were a poet in words, as he is in colours, could not sing, as Wordsworth did, ' I wandered lonely as a cloud.' To him there is no lonely cloud, for it is the dancing feet of the Lord of Love that speed them along the sky.''

Plate LXXVIII, " The Flight of Lakshman Sen," is a very able work by the late Mr. Surendra Nath Ganguly, whose early death cut short a most promising career. It illustrates a well-known

PLATE LXXVIII

THE FLIGHT OF LAKSHMAN SEN

incident in the history of Bengal. The last representative of a long line of famous Brahman kings, surprised in his palace at Nūdīah by Pathān raiders, saves himself by a staircase leading to the river, where the royal barge is waiting.

It is manifestly impossible to do full justice to the New School of Calcutta in a few selected examples by three or four of its artists, though they will suffice to show the reality and sincerity of the revival. The deeper significance of the movement lies, however, not so much in its actual accomplishment, as in the clear evidence it gives of a spiritual resurrection, of the re-awakening of the artistic soul of India from the narcotic slumber, induced by the deadly drugs of a soulless pedagogy, in which there are never dreams of beauty or visions of a fairer world.

Should we take the re-awakening as a challenge or as an inspiration to the Empire?

APPENDIX

THE Indian process of fresco painting as still practised in Rajputana, the Punjab, and the United Provinces, has been lately revived in Bengal by the Calcutta School of Art. Modern fashions and modern bad taste have generally substituted insanitary European wall-papers for this most beautiful and permanent form of Indian mural decoration.

The chief difference between it and the Italian pro-cess of *fresco buono* is that the colours are united to the plaster ground by mechanical action (beating with trowel and polishing) as well as chemically, by the action of the lime. The Indian fresco is given a highly polished surface, which in the dust-laden atmo-sphere of India is a great advantage, as it prevents accumulations of dirt, and enables the wall to be cleaned with a dry duster or by syringing it with water.

For interior decoration the colours are absolutely permanent. The plaster is exceedingly durable, and except when saltpetre (which eventually destroys any lime plaster) rises in the walls it is not affected by a damp atmosphere. In the dry climate of Northern India it was often used for external decoration by the Moguls, and it is quite suitable for this on walls which are not fully exposed to the monsoon rains, or are protected by a verandah.

278

Even when saltpetre rises in the walls, owing to the absence of an effective damp course, it is more durable than common plaster, and it can easily be repaired from time to time. But in this case an upper story, to which the saltpetre does not rise, is more suitable for pictures or for elaborate decorations. For native houses, where the inmates have not adopted the European habit of wearing boots, this plaster is strong enough to be used for floors; and formerly floors were sometimes painted in fresco, which, with its finely polished surface, possessed all the beauty of inlaid marble. The Jaipur lime, owing to its having a large percentage of alumina, makes an exceptionally strong and beautiful plaster.

The Preparation of the Lime for the Ground

The lime must be perfectly slaked to prevent blisters appearing in the ground. It must remain under water for at least a week, though a much longer time is desirable. Then mix with the lime a quantity of powdered limestone, or fine clean sand, double in weight of the dry lime. Stir the mixture, and add water to make it the consistency of mud. Grind the mixture on an ordinary curry-stone. This plaster can be used on brick or rough stone walls. When a wooden ground is used mix the plaster with sugar, powdered *methi* (Trigonell—*fœnum grœcum*), and jute to prevent it from cracking.

The Laying of the Plaster Ground

The stone or brick wall must be well wetted, and while wet the prepared plaster is thinly and evenly laid over it. Drive the plaster well into the joints and crevices, and beat it all over with a long strip of wood used edgeways until it becomes slightly dry. Then wet the layer, and repeat the beating until the plaster is firm. Apply another thin coat of plaster, beating it well in the same way, until it becomes at least a quarter of an inch thick. Then level it carefully and let it dry completely. The operation lasts three or four days.

The Preparation of Lime for Fresco Ground

The lime for the final coating on which the painting is done requires very careful preparation. It must be perfectly slaked, and for this purpose the lime is sometimes kept under water for months; a year is said to be desirable for the very best work. Then curds are mixed with the lime in the proportion of half a seer of curds to half a maund of dry lime. Stir the mixture well, and let it stand under water overnight. Next day drain off the water and strain through a piece of fine cloth. Let it stand again under water till next day, and continue this process for at least a week. The purity of the lime will depend upon the number of times this operation is repeated. Care must be taken that the lime thus prepared is always kept under water; if allowed to dry it will be useless.

The Laying of the Fresco Ground

Wet a portion of this plaster ground prepared as above as much as can be painted and finished in a day. If the ground is too wet it will come off with the rubbing-stone; if insufficiently the ground will dry too quickly and the colours will not be permanent. Then mix some of the plaster of the ground with the fine prepared fresco lime, adding water to make it the consistency of cream, and apply this mixture to the wet wall with a large brush ; rub it well over the ground with a flat stone so as to work it well into the surface. Give two or three coats, rubbing it with the stone every time. Then apply three or four coatings of the prepared fresco lime only, rubbing it as before with the stone. When it is a little dry and sticky polish it with an agate polishing-stone until the surface is quite smooth and glazed ; the ground is then ready for painting. Considerable practice and dexterity are needed in this polishing process.

The process for preparing the beautiful polished white walls which were formerly common in the best houses in Madras and Calcutta, was supposed to be a lost art until I pointed out that it was identical with that used for preparing walls for fresco painting. The walls in Government House, Calcutta, were lately renewed under Lord Curzon's orders by workmen imported from Jaipur for teaching fresco painting in the Calcutta School of Art.

THE PAINTING

The drawing, first carefully made on paper, is transferred to the prepared wall by the usual method of pricking and pouncing the outlines. The colours are mixed with water, ground fine, and strained through a cloth. Gum is added to all the colours except black, which requires glue. The painting must be finished in one day, while the ground is wet, as in the Italian process of *fresco buono* ; but if necessary retouching can be done the following day, provided that the painting is kept wet by covering it with wet cloths. When the painting is finished, beat it all over very evenly with a small thick trowel until the

20

surface is quite smooth. Then scrape the oily liquid from the inside of a cocoa-nut, and, after heating it, apply it to the surface of the painting and rub it gently with a dry, clean cloth. The painting must then be rubbed with a small agate polishing-stone until it acquires a surface like polished marble. When the plaster is thoroughly dry the colours are quite permanent, and the painting can be cleaned from time to time by syringing it with water or dusting it with a dry duster.

COLOURS USED IN JAIPUR FOR REAL FRESCO

Hindustani name.	English.
Hazâ patthar.	Terra verte.
Pilâ patthar.	Yellow ochre.
Lâjward.	Ultramarine (lapis).
Hingûl.	Vermilion.
Sindûr.	Red lead.
Nil.	
Kajâl.	Lampblack.
Koelâ.	Ivory black.
Chûnâ.	Lime.

The following colours can also be used : Raw siena, burnt siena, raw umber, burnt umber, Naples yellow, Venetian red, green oxide of chromium, cobalt blue.

THE AJANTĀ AND SĪGIRI FRESCOES

The ground on which the Ajantā paintings were executed appears to have been composed of pulverised trap, mixed with clay and cow-dung, laid on the roughish surface of the rocks to a depth varying from a quarter to half an inch. Sometimes rice-husks were added, especially on the ceilings. Over this ground was laid the *intonaco* of this smooth plaster, about the thickness of an egg-shell, upon which the painting was done (Mr. John Griffiths, " Ajantā," vol. i, p. 18).

At Sīgiri the ground was a thickness of about half an inch of tempered earth and kaolin of a reddish brown hue, strengthened with rice-husks and perhaps shreds of cocoa-nut fibre. Upon this were laid at least two coatings of white chūnā (lime), a quarter to half an inch thick (Mr. H. C. P. Bell, " Journal R.A.S., Ceylon," vol. xv, p. 114).

NOTES ON INDIAN PAINTING PROCESSES, SUPPLIED BY MR. ISHWARY PRASAD, TEACHER IN THE CAL-CUTTA SCHOOL OF ART

Paper for Miniature Paintings

The papers used were of three kinds : (1) called *bavsāhā*, made from crushed bamboo, (2) *tātāhā*, made from *tāt*, or jute, (3) *tulāt*, made from *tula*, or cotton.

A smooth enamelled surface was given to the paper by placing it face downwards on a polished stone and rubbing the back of it with a polisher.

Tracing Paper (Charba)

This was prepared from deer-skin. Drawings were transferred by pricking and pouncing with charcoal powder. For fine work the charcoal was made from the *arahar* plant (*Cajanus Indicus*) ; for ordinary work charcoal made from mango-tree twigs was used.

Brushes were made from the hair of a squirrel's tail. Worn brushes were carefully kept for fine outline work. Dr. Coomaraswamy says that in Ceylon brushes for drawing fine lines are made of the awns of *teli tana* grass (*Aristida adscensionis*), and are admirably adapted to their purpose.

The first outline was always made with Indian red (*gairika*—a red used by mendicants for colouring their cloths) used without gum. The finishing outlines were made with lampblack, prepared by burning a camphor wick in a mustard-oil lamp.

Mediums.—The mediums used with the colours were water, gum, glue, sugar, and linseed water.

Gold.—The best gold was known as Panna gold, obtained from the Panna State Gold Mines. The gold size was made by boiling fourteen ounces' weight of gum and two ounces' weight of sugar in four ounces of water ; when cold it was ready for use.

The following are the technical names of the principal processes of painting :

Ābina.—Drawing a sketch of the picture with a brush dipped in water only ; the paper, when dry, has a water-line impression which serves as a guide for future work (*ab*—water, *bina*—to see).

Khākā (form).—To give form to the water-line drawing with some mineral colour, Indian red being often used.

Rangamezi (colouring).

(a) *Dagina* (marking).—The different parts of the picture, such as the face, sky, trees, dresses, etc., are marked out with various colours.

(b) *Potna* (filling up).—The spaces thus marked out were filled up with colour-washes.

Golaī.—Gradating and softening of the colours.

Sāyā-susma (shading).

(a) *Sāyā.*—Shading the different parts of the

picture with darker tones. *Sāyā* touches
are only put on the face, hands, feet, folds
of the dress, and accessories such as furniture ; never on the sky or on flat walls.

(b) *Susma.*—To use different colours in giving
relief to an object.

Sia-kalam (ink-brush).—Finishing the whole picture
with ink-lines of varying thickness and strength.

Gula-pamba (chrome yellow and Chinese white).—
This was used instead of gold in painting jewellery,
etc.

Sufāda.—To paint bright spots in the picture, such
as the white of the eye, pearls, and jewellery, with
touches of white.

Jarab.—In this process real pearls and precious
stones were stuck on to the picture (see illustration,
Plate LIV).

Grounds for tempera painting on cloth, wood, and
walls :

Cloth.—For first-class work, boiled and liquefied
khoi (parched paddy) mixed with gum $\frac{1}{16}$ part. For
ordinary work, rice starch mixed with linseed water
$\frac{1}{8}$ part, and gum $\frac{1}{20}$ part.

Wood.—Glue and sugar $\frac{1}{16}$ part, a pinch of alum
and a tablespoonful of shellac, boiled together.

Walls.—Chalk and milk $\frac{1}{2}$ part, milk curd $\frac{1}{8}$, sugar
$\frac{1}{16}$, and a little yellow ochre.

Dr. Waddell, in his " Lamaism in Tibet," p. 331,
describes the method of preparing the ground for the
sacred banners which are hung in Buddhist temples
and monasteries :

" The cloth used is canvas or cotton, seldom silk.
It is prepared by stretching it while damp on a wooden

frame to which a margin of cloth is stitched, and its surface is then smeared with a paste of lime and flour, to which a little glue is sometimes added. On drying the surface is rubbed smooth and slightly polished by a stone, and the drawing is then outlined either by hand or with a charcoal crayon. In the more technical subjects a stencil plate is used."

INDEX

Ajantā, paintings at, 19, 75, 163–173, 224
Akbar's painters, 171, 195–201, 202, 204, 211
Akbar-nāma, 200, 217
Amarāvatī sculptures, 75, 87, 88, 99–108
Ankhor Vat, 114, 137
Anuradhapura, Buddha figure at, 21
Asoka, 74, 88–9, 91, 94
Aurangzīb, 209–10, 229

Bagh, paintings at, 19, 176–7, 195
Baldwin, Mr. Stanley, 70, 255
Bāz Bahādur, 226
Bhagavad Gītā, 43–5
Bhārhut, sculptures at, 82, 92–5
Bichitr, 215, 223–4
Binyon, Mr. Laurence, 5–6, 168
Birdwood, Sir G., 4
Bodhisattvas, images of, 27, 142
Bombay School, 258–9
Boole, George, 59
Borobudur, 21, 22, 109–32, 142
Buddha, image of, 28, 144–5; painting of, 167–70

Calcutta School, 260–77
Calligraphy, 212–13
Cambodia, 114, 138
Chidambaram temple, 42, 65
Chinese painting, 189–91
Chitra-sālas, 156, 193, 262
Cousins, Dr. J. H., 275
Craftsmen, 185–8
Curzon, Lord, 262, 265

Dance of Siva, 31, 57–66, 177
Dārā Shikoh, 209, 219

Delhi, New, 155, 248, 259
Dey, Mr. Mukul Chandra, 167
Dharma, 33, 34
Dharmapāla, image of, 46
Dhyānas, 31
Dhyanī-Buddha, 22, 24
Durgā, image of, 36, 47–8

Education, Indian, 246–8
Elephanta sculptures, 52
Ellora sculptures, 50–3

Fazl, Abul, 195, 196–9, 211, 212
Fergusson, James, 93, 96–7
Foucher, M., 173
Fresco buono, 171–2, *appendix*

Gandhāran art, 12, 20, 21, 25, 27, 28, 106, 107, 141
Ganesha, images of, 66–7
Gangoly, Mr. O. C., 70, 268
Ganguly, Mr. Surendra Nath, 276
Ghiberti gates, 117–18, 123
Ghose, Mr. Asit, 181
Ghulām, 215
Goloubeff, M. Victor, 167, 171
Gothic art, 10, 188–9
Griffiths, Mr. J., 166, 167

Haldar, Mr. Asit Kumar, 177, 275–6
Hashim, Mir, 218
Himalayas, 12–13, 21, 113, 114
Hindu painters, 224–39, 243

Impressionism, Indian, 227–8

Jahāngīr, 201–7, 218–9
Java, sculpture in, 33, 34, 48, 66–7, 143–6
Jouveau-Dubreuil, Professor, 173, 174

287

Kailāsa, Mt., 12–13, 18, 20, 25, 61, 110, 111, 114; temple, 50–52; of the human body, 59–60
Kālī, 36, 181
Kanārak, temple at, 71, 147–8
Kangra school of painting, 178
Kramrisch, Dr., 182
Kutb Shah, Sultan Muhammad, portrait of, 218

Lakhanas, 31
Lecoq, Dr. von, 163

Mahābhārata, 13, 17, 19, 74
Mahā-kundali, 59–60
Mānasarovara, Lake, 13
Manjusri, image of, 36, 47
Manohar, 222
Mansūr, Ustād, 219–22
Mantra, 30
Marshall, Sir John, 71, 171
Mogul paintings, 185–222
Murad, Prince, 215

Nādānta dance, 57–65
Nakhon Vat, 137
Nālanda University, 104–6
Natārāja, 28, 36, 57–65, 70
Nivedita, Sister, 43

Orissan school of sculpture, 147–8; modern, 72–3, 253

Padmapāni, image of, 25–6
" Pat " drawings, 181–2
Peshawar, stūpa at, 20
Prajñāpāramitā, image of, 33
Prambānam sculptures, 135–6

Qudsi, Muhammad Jam, portrait of, 215–16

Rāgas, 30, 31
Rāmāyana, 74
Realism in art, 8, 17, 234–5
Rembrandt, 207–8
Rodin, Auguste, 63, 64

Ronaldshay, Lord, 263, 264, 265, 268
Ruskin, 7, 12, 151

Sānchī sculptures, 57, 95–8
Sankarāchārya, 42, 241
Sarasvati, 30
Shah Jahān, 209, 218
Shāktas, 36–7
Shakti, 29, 30
Shapur of Khurasan, 194–5
Sigiri paintings, 19, 175–6
Sittannavāsal paintings, 173–4
Siva, images of, 27, 28, 34, 35, 42 n., 57–65
Siva-Sīmantinī, 273
Smith, Dr. Vincent, 172
Sudarsana-Chakra, 24–5
Sukrāchārya, 40–1, 140, 140 n.
Swastika dance, 65
Symbolism of colour, 179–181

Tagore, Dr. Abanindra Nath, 72, 172, 238, 260–73
Taine, H., 3, 7–8
Tāj Mahall, 246, 249
Tāla, 30, 31
Tārā, image of, 32–3
Tāranath, history of, 73–8
Tibetan painting, 179
Triangle, symbolism of, 23, 24, 29
Trimūrti, image of, 34

Universities, Indian, 104–6, 247, 248, 256–7

Vajrapāni, image of, 26
Vishnu, 24–5, 36, 53

Woodroffe, Sir John, 36, 260

Yantras, 16, 23–4, 30, 36, 59, 78
Yazdani, Mr. G., 168
Yoga, 10–11, 13, 16, 18, 59–61, 65, 97, 111, 112
Yogi, The Divine, 12, 18, 20, 25, 29, 111

Printed in Great Britain by
Hazell, Watson & Viney, Ld., London and Aylesbury.

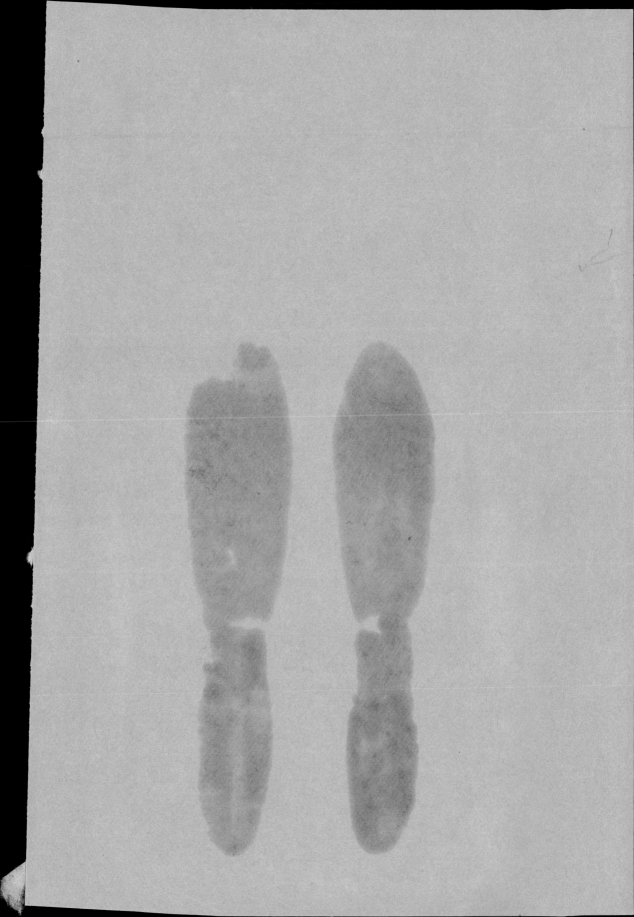

DATE DUE	
DEC 1 3 2013	

GAYLORD　　　　　　　　　　　PRINTED IN U.S.A.